D1281604

THE ARMED FORCES OF ADEN

1839–1967

Cliff Lord and David Birtles

In memory of James Norrie (Jim) Ellis O.B.E.,
without whose help this book would
have remained unpublished

Helion & Company

Helion and Company
26 Willow Road
Solihull
West Midlands
B91 1UE
England
Tel. 0121 705 3393
Fax 0121 711 1315
Email: publishing@helion.co.uk
Website: http://www.helion.co.uk

Published by Helion and Company, 2000
Designed and typeset by Bookcraft Ltd, Stroud, Gloucestershire
Printed by Antony Rowe Ltd., Chippenham, Wiltshire
Limited edition printing of 500 numbered copies. This is copy no. **416**

A supplement volume to this book is already in preparation, and the publishers
would be pleased to hear from any reader who believes they can contribute
relevant material.

© Helion and Company 2000

ISBN 1 874622 40 X

British Library Cataloguing-in-Publication Data
A catalogue record for this book is available from the British Library.

All rights reserved. No part of this publication may be reproduced, stored in a
retrieval system, or transmitted, in any form, or by any means, electronic,
mechanical, photocopying, recording or otherwise, without the express written
consent of Helion and Company.

For details of other military history titles published by Helion and Company contact
the above address, or visit our website: http://www.helion.co.uk.

We always welcome receiving proposals from prospective authors working in
military history.

Contents

Directory of Units

Appendices

Acknowledgements

Captain Jim Ellis, O.B.E., and last Resident Adviser in the Eastern Aden Protectorate, provided a detailed analysis of all the military forces in the Eastern Aden Protectorate. Major General J.D. Lunt C.B.E., provided an overview of the military forces of Aden during his time, and Brigadier J.H. Mallard wrote about his Federal National Guard. Maj. Charles R. Butt kept in contact for many years sending both photographs and information regarding his A.P.L. days. An Aden Police perspective was provided by F.W. (Dicky) Bird, M.B.E., G.M. Continued support from Tom Wylie, with his photographs and keen interest, kept the authors on track. Dr. Huub Driessen and Sqn. Ldr. Rana Chhina I.A.F. (Retd.) provided historical research from London and New Delhi. The maps were prepared by cartographer Frank Bailey of Waikato University, and the rank illustrations were drawn by Malcolm Thomas. The appendices on Arabian Medals and Awards were drawn up by Owain Raw-Rees, an expert in this field. Of special mention is Aaron Fox who provided information on weapons, advice, and support in many different areas.

Even with their assistance, the authors still owe a great debt of gratitude to many other people and organisations for their assistance, information, and help. Many served in Aden and the Protectorates, and have written giving details of their service, and provided historical and uniform details of their units. Without their contributions this book would never have been written. They are: A.H.B.5 (R.A.F.), Room 411, Ministry of Defence, London; Raymond Butler; J.B. Claro, M.O.D. Naval Historical Branch, London; Peter Cooke; Bill Cranston; Michael Crouch; R.H. Daly; Stephen Day; John Daymond; D.C.L.I. Museum, Bodmin; Defence Equipment Administration, Crown Agents, Sutton; Department of Photographs, Imperial War Museum, London; Departmental Record Officer (Archives), Ministry of Defence, London; Deputy Keeper, Department of Printed Books, Imperial War Museum, London; Directorate of Public Relations (Army), Ministry of Defence, London; James Dunn; Wing Commander E.I. Elliott; P.J.V. Elliott, Keeper of Research and Information Services, Royal Air Force Museum, Honington; Fa'iz Fattah; S. Folkes, Reader Services, The British Library, Oriental and India Office Collections, London; R.A. Hale; J. Bryant Haigh; J.G.R. Harding; M. Harding, Department of Archives, Photographs, Film and Sound, National Army Museum, London; E. Haynes; Royal Artillery Historical Trust, Woolwich; Glen Hodgins; S.K. Hopkins, Department of Uniform, National Army Museum, London; Edward Horne B.E.M.; R.W. Howes, Official Publications Library, The British Library, London; K.G.F. Irwin; A.H. Lawes,

Search Department, Public Record Office, Kew; I.S. Lockhart, Records Branch, Foreign and Commonwealth Office, London; J. Longworth, Army Historical Branch, Ministry of Defence, London; Anthony N. McClenaghan; Michael McKeown; Steve Marriott, Police Insignia Collectors Association of Great Britain; Oliver Miles; Todd Mills; Ashok Nath; Photographic Section, Public Record Office, Kew; R.H.Q. P.W.R.R., Canterbury; A.H.H. Richardson, Library and Records Department, Foreign and Commonwealth Office, London; Royal Engineers Museum, Chatham; Royal Hampshire Regiment Museum, Winchester; Royal Signals Museum, Blandford Forum; David A. Ryan; W. Stroud, Librarian, *Soldier*, The British Army Magazine; Frank Stevens; A. Thomas, A.H.B. (R.A.F.), Room 308, Ministry of Defence, London; Major General "Sandy" Thomas C.B., D.S.O., M.C.; Rex Trye.

Photographs

The authors wish to thank the many people who loaned their photographs so they could be included in this book. Special thanks go to the Royal Signals, and *Soldier Magazine* for permission to use their photographs, and David Belson, Crown Copyright Administrator, Ministry of Defence, London for his assistance.

Authors' Note

For those that served in Aden with locally raised forces it is always disappointing to find that their unit rarely gets a mention in any publication. The authors have tried to rectify this by offering a perspective that focuses on the locally raised units that were a permanent feature of the armed forces of Aden. Both Indian Army and British Army units were raised in Aden, and these are also included; however they are not described in as much detail. A general overview of the many regiments that served in Aden during times of crisis is included in the appendices.

While writing this book it quickly became evident that South Arabian place names lacked a standardised spelling. Over the years a village may have many different spellings of its name on maps and in books. The authors hope the reader will indulge them by accepting the spelling provided.

Foreword

Captain J.N. Ellis, O.B.E., D.S.M. (Qu'aiti)
Resident Adviser, Eastern Aden Protectorate 1965–1967

Because of its strategic position, Aden has a long and momentous history as an international port, having a magnificent natural harbour at the junction of the Red Sea and the Indian Ocean. The harbour attracted the British, and Captain S.B. Haines of the Indian Marine, the East India Company's Navy, occupied Aden in January 1839. This book is confined to the military history of the British era, which lasted until 29th November 1967. Special attention has been given to the Arab units raised in Aden and the Protectorate. The authors both served with Arab troops in and around Aden and the protectorates in the 1960s and have taken upon themselves the considerable task of researching and collating the material, a work which no one else has attempted in detail. Indeed they have provided us with a work of historical as well as specialist value.

Jim Ellis
27 April 1999

Introduction

When Britain left South Arabia in 1967 it marked the end of an era. It was more than just losing another country to independence – it finalised the end of frontier-style soldiering. Although a part of the Arabian Peninsular, there were many links with India. Aden and the Protectorate had been administered by the Bombay Presidency in India until 1937 when it became a colony under the control of the Colonial Office in London.

In the nineteenth century the port of Aden became famous because of its strategic value at the southern-most point of the Red Sea. It was used as a major refuelling station by naval and merchant shipping prior to their departure across the Indian Ocean or journey north to the Suez Canal. Britain had seized the sleepy Arabian town of Aden in 1839 to protect its vital interests in the area, and signed treaties with the various sheikhs and sultans who laid claim to the adjacent coastal lands. These areas were to become known as the Protectorate, later being divided into the Eastern and Western Aden Protectorates for administrative purposes. Each state had its own local military forces for protection, whilst Britain provided advice and external security. The Protectorate was a collection of states in which emirs, sultans and sheikhs ruled their subjects with absolute authority. *Felix* Arabia was a place where time had stood still for centuries. Peaceful Arabia it had been, but that was destined to change.

The wind of change sweeping through Africa in the late 1950s also blew across the Gulf of Aden to the Colony and Protectorate. There was little that could be done to prevent the onward march of Arab nationalism. Politicians in Britain deemed it necessary to bring all the individual states of the Protectorate into a single federation. In 1959 six of the states in the Western Aden Protectorate united as the Federation of the Amirates of the South, a name that was changed to the Federation of South Arabia when Aden Colony joined in 1963. Most of the States in the Western Aden Protectorate eventually joined the Federation, as well as Wahidi State from the Eastern Aden Protectorate. With the advent of federation, the political situation in the country deteriorated. Opposition came from the South Arabian League, National Liberation Front and the Front for the Liberation of South Yemen. In 1966 the British announced that their troops would withdraw by 31 December 1968, a statement which immediately triggered a power struggle between the rival factions. Attacks on Government forces increased. Loyalties were reviewed by one and all, and the collapse of the Federation became inevitable. The partially-realised hope of a united South Arabia was shattered by a tortuous civil war, which brought the fledgling Federation and the states of the Eastern Aden Protectorate into one country – The People's Republic of South Yemen.

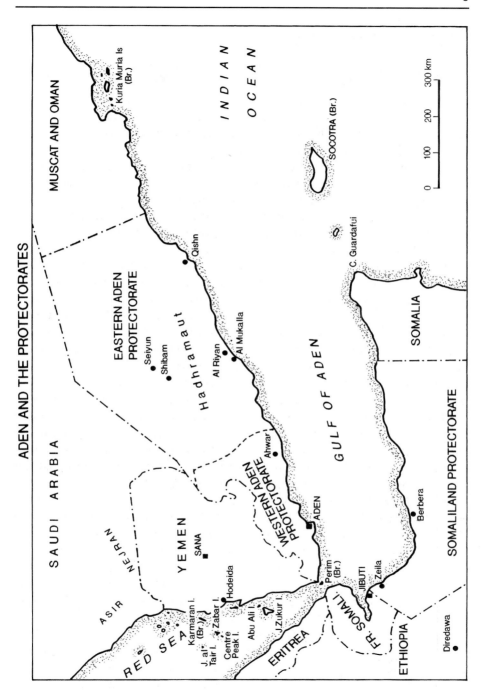

ADEN AND THE PROTECTORATES

10

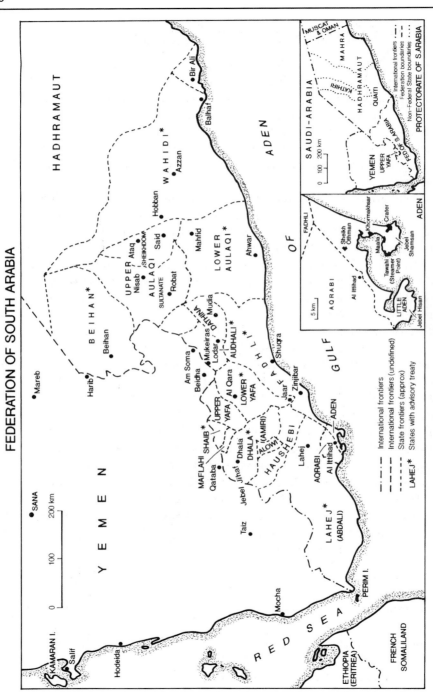

FEDERATION OF SOUTH ARABIA

HADHRAMAUT

Bir Ali

Balhaf

ADEN

WAHIDI *

Azzan

Hobban

Mahfid

UPPER Atag

Said

Nisab /SHEIKHDOM

AULAQI

SULTANATE

Robat

LOWER

AULAQI *

Ahwar

GULF

Mudia

UPPER YAFA-JIHA

AUDHALI *

Shuqra

Am Soma

Mukeiras

Loda

Beidha

Al Qara *

Zinjibar

LOWER

YAFA

Jaar

DHALA

ADEN

Mareb

UPPER

YAFA

MAFLAHI *

(AMIRI)

SHAIB *

Harib

Qataba Jihaf Dhala

(ALOWI)

BEIHAN *

Jebel

DHALA *

HAUSHEBI

Beihan

Lahej

AQRABI

SANA

Al Ittihad

200 km

LAHEJ *

(ABDALI)

100

Taiz

YEMEN

0

Mocha

PERIM I.

KAMARAN I.

Salif

RED SEA

Hodeida

ETHIOPIA

(ERITREA)

FRENCH

SOMALILAND

International frontiers

International frontiers (undefined)

State frontiers (approx)

States with advisory treaty

LAHEJ *

MUSCAT & OMAN

MAHRA

SAUDI-ARABIA

KATHIRI

HADHRAMAUT

QUAITI

International frontiers

Federation boundaries

Non-Federal State boundaries

PROTECTORATE OF S.ARABIA

200 km

100

0

YEMEN

UPPER YAFA

FED.OF S.ARABIA

ADEN

FADHLI

Khormakhsar

Sheikh Othman

Crater

AQRABI

Maala

Jebel

Tewahi

Shamsan

(Steamer Point)

Al Ittihad

LITTLE ADEN

5 km

Jebel Hisan

The Capture of Aden

Communication between Britain and India was exceedingly slow in the nineteenth century because ships were required to travel via the Cape of Good Hope. In order to shorten the time that despatches could be passed between Bombay and London, various overland routes were tried. One of these was the Alexandria to Suez pony-express. Consequently the Red Sea route became popular and a need arose for a refuelling station. Aden was considered as it is situated about half-way between Suez and Bombay, and possessed an excellent sheltered port.

Negotiations were conducted between Commander Haines, Political Agent of the Bombay Government, and the Sultan of Lahej, the owner of Aden, for the port and environs. An agreement was made, but when it came to executing that agreement the Sultan's son refused. At this time a Madras ship, the *Duria Dowlat*, under British colours, was wrecked near Aden, and the survivors were mistreated by the local Arabs whilst the cargo was plundered. This and the insults that had been heaped upon Haines and Britain by the Lahej Sultan were enough to cause the Bombay Government to send some ships of the Honourable East Indies Company Navy to take the "Rock" of Aden by force.

The ships sent were the Honourable East Indies Company's sloop of war *Coote*, schooner *Mahi*, and barque *Anne Crichton*. Two Royal Navy vessels and troop transports were despatched from India to join Commander Haines. They were H.M.S. *Volage*, H.M. Brig *Cruiser* and the transports *Lowjee Family* and *Ernaad*, which arrived on 16th January 1839. The troops on board were: The Bombay European Regiment; 24th Regiment Bombay Native Infantry; 4th Company of the 1st Battalion Artillery; and 6th Company (Golundauze) Artillery. Ten garrison guns were included for the defence of the port.

After a naval bombardment had silenced the Arab guns Aden was captured on 19th January 1839. With this successful action, Britain gained its first new territory under Queen Victoria. Aden was annexed as part of the Bombay Presidency. It also marked the beginning of a permanent military garrison. In May 1840 that garrison consisted of:

2 Battalion Artillery
Golundauze Battalion
Engineer Corps
H.M. 6th Regiment
Bombay European Regiment
10th Regiment Native Infantry
16th Regiment Native Infantry

During the first few years following the capture of Aden there were several attempts by the Arabs to recapture it. On each occasion the military garrison, with the help of the Red Sea Squadron of the Indian Navy, succeeded in repulsing the attacking tribesmen.

In 1858 a force composed of 2 or 3 companies of 57th Regiment, a wing of the 29th Bombay Infantry and a detachment from the Hon. Company's Ship *Elphinstone*, defeated an Arab force at Sheikh Othman. Britain was now secure in Aden although a few further military actions took place.

The first of these was the Expedition to Shugra in December 1865 when trouble was experienced with the Fadhli tribe. The tribe had plundered a caravan within gunshot of the Aden fortifications. A detachment of 300 men of the 101st Grenadiers with a field force commanded by Colonel Woollcombe, C.B., Royal Artillery, attacked Bir and Asala, destroying the latter. They returned to Aden on 9 January 1866. Another expedition under the same commander was sent to Shugra on 14 March to destroy the town and forts, which was the principal stronghold of the Fadhli tribe. The Fadhli had captured a dhow under British protection, massacred the crew, and sold the cargo. The British believed the Fadhli needed to be taught a lesson and a detachment of artillery, with two field pieces, and three companies of the 109th Infantry Regiment and some sappers were despatched by H.M.S. *Lyra* and *Victoria*. The seamen and marines from the *Lyra*, about 40 in number, worked with the artillery. The town was destroyed on 15 March and the troops were back in Aden the following day.

A few years later, 1873, a force of British and Indian infantry with three guns marched to Al Hauta (Lahej) to protect the Sultan against the Turks who had invaded his territory. After negotiations the Turkish troops were withdrawn.

Directory of Units

1st Yemen Infantry

Turkish troops based at Lahej during the First World War posed a serious threat to the port of Aden, and a Movable Column of British and Indian troops was employed in harassing the Turkish force. Captain M.C. Lake (later Lieutenant Colonel Lake, C.M.G., O.B.E.) of the 101st Grenadiers organised a band of tribal irregulars for skirmishing and intelligence gathering in 1915. They patrolled the area of land between Sheikh Othman and the Turkish garrison in Lahej with great success, perhaps because they were more suited to the environment than the other Allied forces in the area. This irregular tribal band was regularised as the 1st Yemen Infantry in 1918, and was fully operational by 1919. Recruited from local tribes, the force was approximately 400 men strong, although over 1,000 names appear on the medal roll for the British War and Victory medals. The unit was based at Sheikh Othman in the vacated Aden

Officers and British N.C.O.'s of the 1st Yemen Infantry, c.1920. The officer commanding, Captain M.C. Lake appears in the second row, second from left. The tall officer in the centre is Lt. Pearce, later Captain, Queen's Royal West Surrey Regiment. The R.S.M. appears on the far left of the front row. (Bill Cranston)

Troop accommodation. Colonel Meinhertzhagen inspected the force in 1923 and reported that their military value was nil. As a consequence of his report, the unit was disbanded in 1925.

British officers and men wore a solar *topee* with a diamond flash on the left-hand side with the words YEMEN 1st INFANTRY, in white, in three tiers. Brass metal shoulder titles with the same words as the *topee* flash were also worn. Arab soldiers and officers wore their own distinctive khaki turban with a plain coloured flash on the left-hand side. All ranks wore a khaki tunic and shorts, with a leather belt. Soldiers wore a leather bandolier, while officers wore a Sam Browne. All Arabs and British Warrant Officers and Senior Non-Commissioned Officers wore full-length puttees.

23 (Fortress) Company, Royal Bombay Sappers and Miners

In 1900 the Bombay Sappers and Miners included a service company in Aden. It appears that this service company was replaced by a fortress company in 1902 as no further reference to it in Aden is mentioned in Sandes' *The Indian Sappers and Miners*. By 1903 the Fortress Company was renamed 23 (Fortress) Company, 3rd Sappers and Miners and was located in Aden. 23rd (Fortress) Company, Royal Bombay Sappers and Miners, as it became known in 1921, remained in Aden until disbanded in 1928.

45 (Aden) Rifles

An infantry unit known as the Aden Rifles was formed on 1 January 1917 by Army Department notification number 1588 of 1916. With an establishment of one reserve company, this unit was reconstituted as an Indian Defence Force unit, with the designation of 45 (Aden) Rifles from 1 April 1917. This volunteer force was raised from the local population and a small number of British officers, for the defence of Aden during the First World War. Senior officers of the Company were Major Harold Berridge O.B.E. and Major James Bett Grey, who became the Commandant. Major Berridge was attached to the Royal Engineers. With the general demobilisation and down-scaling of forces in the Indian Army, the company was disestablished in 1920. Although some sources indicate the unit existed until 1934, this was probably on paper only.

410 Rifleman S.O. Whitley, 45th Aden Rifles, Indian Defence Force, was awarded Mentioned in Despatches (Aden Field Force G.G.O. 1747, dated 27 August 1920).

90 Company R.A.S.C.

Raised on 1 December 1957, in Aden, this unit was largely composed of locally enlisted staff. The role of the unit was to supply staff cars and administrative vehicles for Middle East Command and the various other units in the Aden Garrison. With the run-down of British Troops in Aden due to the withdrawal the unit moved to Sharjah.

1401 (Aden) Company, Pioneer Corps

In 1940, two Pioneer Corps companies were raised in Aden to provide labour for the Somaliland Campaign. Tasks involved road maintenance, airfield construction and port operation. Generally pioneer companies were of no fixed size, but usually were between 100 and 500 men. Although independent and self-sufficient, the companies were clustered into Groups for administrative purposes. Most foreign companies were unarmed.

On 2 November 1940 British staff arrived at Tawahi to raise 1401 (Aden) Company. By the end of January 1941 the total strength of locally recruited men was 574. Because of the good response to recruiting, the officer commanding, Major J.V.L. Kell of the South Staffordshire Regiment, decided to raise another company, 1402 (Aden) Company. Major Kell was then appointed to command the Group, which was responsible for 1401–1419 Companies. Major Kell was later replaced by Captain D.N. Seton of The Welch Regiment.

The company sailed from Aden on 14 March 1941. Troops disembarked from their transport at Berbera two days later in small boats. They formed up on the foreshore at the rear of the infantry, and then moved up to Berbera town in field formation. The sight of so many troops advancing on the town, even though the pioneers were unarmed, was enough for the Italian garrison to put up only minimal resistance before quickly decamping. Berbera was soon captured, and the company commenced construction of a road to the pier, and provided working parties to unload lighters. After this successful campaign, the company returned to Aden on 16 April 1941, and disbanded on 21 May. The uniform was simply khaki shorts and shirts.

1402 (Aden) Company, Pioneer Corps

The company was formed on 1 February 1941, from the surplus of 1401 Company, and was commanded by Captain S.H.J. Harrison, Royal Sussex Regiment. Initially 100 men were employed with the R.A.F. at the aerodrome in Aden. On 14 March 1941 the unit embarked at Aden for Berbera, with 1

British officer, 3 British other ranks, 1 Arab officer and 185 Arab other ranks. Bombardment of the town of Berbera by the Aden Striking Force commenced at about 0435 hrs on 16 March. At daybreak the company remained on board the troop transport *Chakdina* to assist with unloading cargo which was required for the attack. Later, the company was employed in levelling ground for an aerodrome and also worked on the pier road and various other duties for the Engineers and Ordnance Corps. After this successful tour in Somaliland, the company returned to Aden on 14 April, and was disbanded there a week later.

1422 (Sultan Saleh's Hadramaut) Company, Pioneer Corps

On 27 March 1943 Captain D.N. Seton, of The Welch Regiment, was instructed to form a new pioneer company in Aden. A number of British other ranks from the Aden Protectorate Levies were selected and posted to the unit. 2 Arab subalterns also joined the force, which consisted of six sections of 25 men. On 17 July 1943, the company arrived by ship at the port of Mukalla in the Eastern Aden Protectorate, where the unit was employed on road construction. Once the work was completed, the unit returned to Aden on 3 December 1943. Three days later they embarked for the island of Socotra to relieve 2004 Company, where the company was involved with unloading petrol and road construction until the end of January 1944. It is believed that the unit was disbanded shortly after the work was completed.

Aden Defence Light Section, Indian Submarine Corps

In 1899 Major A.M. Stuart, R.E., began developing a system of electric light defence for the Indian ports. As a consequence of his efforts a section consisting of 1 British officer, 2 Mechanists and 6 other ranks (R.E.), with 4 Indian mechanics, was authorised for the maintenance of the electric defence lights, telegraphs and telephones at Aden. Affiliation with the 3rd Bombay Sappers and Miners took place in 1910. In 1912 the Indian Submarine Corps was abolished and the units were known as Defence Light Sections. The Aden Defence Light Section was amalgamated into 23 (Fortress) Company in 1927. 23 (Fortress) Company disbanded in 1928.

Aden Police

Shurtah al Adn

Troops of Aden Police existed as early as 1857. By 1928 the Aden Police were under the control of a Deputy Superintendent of the Bombay Provincial Police Department. Their task was conventional policing within the metropolitan area of Aden. The existence of one British and one Indian infantry battalion was of sufficient moral effect to prevent any trouble, as the battalions could be used to support the Aden Police.

With the change of responsibility for defence from Army to R.A.F., both battalions of infantry were removed, which consequently necessitated an improvement in the organization of the existing police force. In addition, the police force needed to be brought up to strength, as well requiring a certain amount of reorganization. It was soon realized that a force of armed police was necessary to furnish the moral support previously provided by the army battalions. Accordingly, the Government of India and the Government of Bombay tasked two police officers from the Indian Police Service to proceed to Aden, study the reorganization of the Civil Police, and examine the scheme for the recruitment of armed police. Reports submitted in July 1928 recommended that the force should be organized as a whole under a District Superintendent of Police and an Assistant Superintendent. This would replace the Assistant Resident in charge of the Police, and the Deputy Superintendent in immediate charge. The majority of the proposals were accepted, and the establishment was set at 2 British officers, 14 inspectors, 4 *Jamadars* (a rank which may be described as the Indian equivalent of Assistant Sub-Inspector), 200 Armed Police, 292 constables and 13 clerks.

The Government of India regarded the local recruitment of the Armed Police as an experiment. Pending their local recruitment and training it was decided to employ an interim force of 115 Armed Police recruited from India, and men from the earlier disbanded Aden Troop. This force was not to be withdrawn until it was clear that the locally raised Armed Police were fully efficient and capable of carrying out the duties entrusted to them. The Interim Police came into being on 9 January 1929, followed by the recruitment and training of the Permanent Armed Police, and the reorganization of the Civil Police. The Superintendent of Police was a British officer of the Indian Police Service. He had sole charge of the Aden Police Force, Armed and Unarmed, and control of the detachment of the Armed Police in Perim Island and the Kamaran Islands. His uniform was that of the Indian Police. Accommodation for the Interim Force was at the infantry barracks in Crater, Aden. The Interim Force proved its worth and lasted until December 1931. That same year the newly formed

Aden Armed Police marching with fixed bayonets, c.1937. Note the Indian influence, represented by the style of headdress. Aden was a dependency of the Indian Government until 1937, when it became a crown colony. (David Birtles)

Armed Police replaced the Aden Protectorate Levies platoon at Kamaran. There were disturbances in Crater between Arabs and Jews in 1932 which lasted several days, and the Armed Police were called out to patrol the streets, and to restore law and order.

When Aden became a Crown Colony in 1937, the Aden Police retained responsibility for the Colony and the islands of Perim and Kamaran. The Colonial Reports' Annual of 1938 lists the following Unarmed Police: 232 Aden Land and Sheikh Othman Foot Police, 12 Perim Land Police, 13 Sheikh Othman Mounted Police and 62 Aden Harbour Police. In Aden there were 141 Armed Police, in addition to 33 on Perim Island, and 31 at Kamaran. The Armed Police also provided military guards at Government House and manned road blocks when necessary. They were armed with .303 Lee Enfield rifles, and in later years, 9mm Sterling machine carbines.

During the Second World War, a Temporary Additional Constabulary was added to the Service. After the War the Civil Police grew in size, and included the following sections: Uniformed Police Section; Traffic Section; Marine Police Section; Prison Department; Criminal Investigation Department;

Special Branch; Police Band; Fire Brigade. The Aden Police became a part of the South Arabian Police on 1 June 1967.

The uniform issue for the Police during the 1930s was as follows:

1 pair of putties, 2 pairs shorts, 2 shirts, 1 pair *chaplis*, 1 monogram A.P., 1 Fez cap, 1 baton with hook, 1 whistle, 1 belt and buckle plate. The Armed Police were also issued with black boots.

Later that decade the uniform was to change and included:

1 *kullah*, 1 *pugri*, 2 shirts, 2 pairs shorts, 1 pair putties, 1 pair *chaplis* and 1 *durrie*. Equipment consisted of 1 water bottle with carrier, 1 haversack, 1 belt, 1 buckle plate, 1 bandolier leather, 1 pouch, 1 frog.

From 1938 gazetted officers wore their uniform based on the Dress Regulations for Colonial Police Service (C.P.S.) dated May 1938. The Aden Police hat badge was worn on the police cap, and on the front of the Wolseley-pattern helmet under a dark blue silk 8-fold *puggaree*. Collar badges, which depicted the badge of the colony on a shield, were worn on the full-dress and undress tunic collar. Mess dress collar badges were of sterling silver. Those badges worn on a khaki collar had a dark blue background of Melton cloth cut to the shape of the badge. All metal buttons were C.P.S. pattern, viz. the Imperial Crown and a wreath surrounding the monogram C.P.S., and embodying the motto SALUS POPULI. Buttons came in four sizes, and were chromium plated on nickel silver, except for those for mess dress, which were of silver.

The cap badge of the Police Force was the badge of the colony in white metal, encircled with the inscription ADEN POLICE in English and ADN in Arabic. The whole was surmounted by the Tudor Crown, which was replaced with the St Edward's Crown after 1953. An officer's-quality badge was issued after 1953, which was similar to the existing badge, but with the addition of blue enamel. At the same time new collar badges – which were a smaller version of the cap badge – were introduced. They were issued in white metal, voided white metal and silver. Chrome buttons with the force device were also worn after 1953.

Other ranks wore white metal titles with the letters A P on the epaulettes of their shirts. Each policeman's number was stamped on the white metal clasp of his leather belt. The clasp had the words ADEN POLICE above the crown and the number below the crown.

By 1967 the uniform of the Civil Police consisted of: khaki drill uniform with a blue *tarboosh*, blue hosetops, putties and black boots. Marine Police wore a white shirt and shorts, with the blue *tarboosh*. Traffic Police wore a khaki drill uniform with white sleeves, a blue peaked cap with a white cover, and blue hose tops and boots. The Fire Brigade wore a blue drill uniform of

Aden Armed Police, in ceremonial dress, on guard at Government House, Aden, 1952. (Hugh Walker)

Aden Police constable, Khormaksar, 1957. He wears blue hosetops and *chaplis* without socks. Note the dark blue lanyard evident over his left shoulder. (David Birtles)

trousers, a jacket with a double row of buttons, and a blue cap. NCOs and constables had leather belts with large white metal buckles.

For ceremonial occasions Armed Police wore a khaki drill uniform with a red Punjabi-style *pagri* with a *shamla*. A red cummerbund, and red hosetops with puttees and black boots were also worn. Working dress consisted of a khaki drill uniform with a blue beret, blue hosetops, puttees and black boots.

Immediately after the departure of the British from Aden the cap badge was modified by the simple expedient of cutting the crown from the top of the badge.

Aden Protectorate Levies
Jaish Mahmayat Adn

A squadron of R.A.F. bombers arrived at Khormaksar airfield just outside Aden in 1928. They were the tangible result of a decision made in April 1927 when Aden became an Air Command. The doctrine of air control would remain in force for the next thirty years.

Prior to 1928, the garrison in Aden consisted mainly of a small number Sappers and Miners, Royal Artillery and one British and one Indian infantry battalion. However, by 1927 trouble was stirring in the Western Aden Protectorate. It was estimated that a divisional-sized military force was required to contain the problem, and it was successfully argued that air power could do the job for a fraction of the price. This innovative idea worked well in the short term. To secure the airfields a body of men was raised on 1 April 1928. Known as the Aden Protectorate Levies (A.P.L.), they were also available to assist the civil police when required.

The A.P.L. were recruited mainly from the Western Aden Protectorate tribes. Colonel M.C. Lake, of the Indian Army, became the first commanding officer of a unit which consisted of 2 British officers and six platoons of Arab infantry. The Arab officers held governor's commissions. The unit had 8 mules and 48 camels on its strength. Since Aden was administered by the Bombay Presidency until 1937, it was more strongly influenced by New Delhi than London. For example, the A.P.L. had a strong Indian Army stamp on it. A number of senior N.C.O.'s and junior officers were Indian. Even the headdress was a Punjabi-style turban, rather than the traditional Arab *imama*. Having set

Aden Armed Police on parade at Crater Barracks, Aden, 1965. The officer taking the salute wears a khaki uniform and black peaked cap and shoes. Socks are khaki with blue turnovers. Leading the parade is an Arab officer wearing red ceremonial turban, and blue hosetops with red turnover. The rank and file wear blue hosetops and tarbooshes. The entire parade wears khaki tunics and shorts, and a black leather belt with police buckle. (F.W. Bird)

up the levies, Colonel Lake handed over command in 1929 to Lieutenant-Colonel J.C. Robinson D.S.O., who remained in command for ten years. One of the platoons was converted to a Machine Gun Camel Troop, which became mechanised in 1938.

To provide cover from air attack, an anti-aircraft wing was formed by 1939, and during the Second World War an Italian plane was shot down. During the war the strength of the levies increased from 600 to 1,600 men, and they provided garrisons in Socotra Island and Sharjah, in addition to their other duties in the Western Aden Protectorate and Aden Colony. Establishment increases in 1942 provided for R.H.Q., headquarters company, training company, anti-aircraft battery, signal company and ten rifle companies. In April 1943 the garrison at Socotra was increased to three companies, and two 75mm field guns for anti-submarine defence were added. By 1946 the complement of the levies had risen to over 1,800 men.

By 1948 Royal Air Force Regiment officers and airmen had replaced army personnel, a process which had started as early as 1942. As a consequence of this new policy, the A.P.L. became organised as a tactical force of two wings, each about the size of an infantry battalion, and an administration wing. This later became three wings, each of three infantry squadrons. 10 Squadron was established as an armoured car unit using Ferret Mark II scout cars, and consisted entirely of R.A.F. personnel. Members of 10 Squadron were distinguished from all other airmen by their unique cap badge, the A.P.L. insignia of crossed *jambias* on a R.A.F. beret. This was not an authorised badge but a locally-made emblem which was accepted within the command. When the army replaced the R.A.F. in 1957, the armoured car squadron was gradually re-staffed by Arab troops. A hospital for the levies was established along with a medical wing.

During 1952 and 1953 Saudi Arabian interest in the Burami Oasis caused the A.P.L. to provide support for the Trucial Oman Levies. The A.P.L. succeeded in their military task but then mutinied, murdering two of their officers, and returned to Aden in disgrace. From 1947 onwards there was much turmoil within the Western Aden Protectorate, and A.P.L. were frequently in action. In 1954 an A.P.L. convoy sent to relieve a remote fort was ambushed in the Wadi Hatib and suffered many casualties.

In 1957 administration of the levies changed when the War Office assumed control. R.A.F. personnel moved out and were replaced by British army officers and a fourth battalion of infantry was formed. With headquarters at Seedaseer Lines, Khormaksar, there were "up country" bases at Dhala, Mukeiras, Beihan and occasional out-stations at Zinjibar, Lodar and Ataq. In 1958 the levies, supported by the Shropshire Light Infantry and the R.A.F., fought off a strong force of Yemeni troops and dissident tribesmen on the Jebel Jihaf, driving them

Officers of the Aden Protectorate Levies, 1932. Left to right, front row: R.S.M., unknown, senior R.A.F. officer, Lt.Col. Robinson D.S.O., Col. M.C. Lake, Capt. E. Hamilton, Ahmad Salih Maqtaria; left to right, back row: D.J. Hassama, Dr Bashiri, Salim Islam Azzani, Hanash Ahmed Aulaqi, Capt. Fazal Ahmed B.E.M., Al Khader Mohsin Aulaqi. (Lt.Col. Nadir Ali, M.B.E.)

A.P.L. Camel Section, c.1937. The officer's headdress is a solar *topee*. The levies wear their distinctive *mashedda* and *khulla*. All have a green flash with white horizontal bar and green fringe. (David Birtles)

R.A.F. armoured car and lorry used in Aden during the 1930s and '40s (British Crown Copyright/M.O.D.)

A.P.L. man a 40mm quick-firing Bofors AA gun during the Second World War (British Crown Copyright/M.O.D.)

back over the Yemen border.

During the late 1950s operations focused on border hostilities with the Yemen, and were similar in style to operations on the Indian Frontier. Good picquetting drill was essential for survival. The Yemenis often crossed the border for "shoot-up raids", a murder, or just cattle rustling. Weapons used by the A.P.L. were mainly the .303 Rifle No. 4 Mk I, 3 inch Mortar and Bren Guns. Vickers Medium Machine Guns were also used in more static environments. Good wireless communications enabled the A.P.L. to call in R.A.F. support, which consisted of rocket-firing Venoms and Shackleton Mk1 bombers. The bombers would make a stately run, dropping bombs and firing machine guns as well. In theory, casualty evacuation by air could be provided by R.A.F. Sycamore helicopters. Mukeiras and Dhala camps were often shot-up at night, as were resupply convoys for the Government Guard fort at Marta'a (Merta).

By the end of the decade support and ancillary units included a very capable signal squadron, an R.A.F.-run hospital, 10 Armoured Car Squadron equipped with Ferrets and Saladins, a Royal Artillery battery, and a training battalion of the A.P.L. A Camel Company was retained, although it was later used for ceremonial occasions only.

With the creation of the Federation of Amirate of the South, the Aden Protectorate Levies were eventually renamed the Federal Regular Army on 30 November 1961, and changed their allegiance from Queen Elizabeth to the Federation.

Discipline in the A.P.L. was generally good, but there was a tendency for desertion or going absent without leave, because a man's real loyalty was to his tribe, village, family or clan. If he was not able to get leave whenever required then he would take "French leave" so as to play his part in the family, tribal disputes or harvesting, after which he would return to his military duty.

The soldier was armed with a Rifle, No.4 Mk I, which he was permitted to keep when discharged. A modern rifle, in a country where the rifle was the mark of a man, was indeed worth soldiering for.

When "up-country" the uniform of the Arab A.P.L. troops consisted of khaki drill shirts and shorts, grey woollen socks rolled down to the ankles, and brown canvas shoes. The headdress was a simple roll of khaki cloth, worn over the head in a style known as an Audhali turban. The name comes from the type of headdress worn by the Audhali tribe, which provided much of the manpower for the A.P.L. British soldiers had a similar "up-country" uniform, except that they wore khaki drill slacks and suede desert boots, and often wore locally-made ammunition belts of soft leather, instead of the cotton bandoleers. These locally-made belts had 55 loops for individual bullets, and a carrying strap for the *jambia*, which was the preferred equipment of the Arab

26

A.P.L. *jundies* show off the various orders of dress, c.1950. The khaki shirt has no collar and only one pocket, on the left-hand side. The sandals are locally-made. (British Crown Copyright/ M.O.D.)

A.P.L. camel mortar section, c.1950. The weapon is a British 3" mortar with Mk.III mounting. (British Crown Copyright/M.O.D.)

A.P.L. armoured car. These initially had R.A.F. crews, but were later used by Arab soldiers. The R.A.F. crews wore berets with the unofficial A.P.L. *jambia* badge. (British Crown Copyright/M.O.D.)

A.P.L. bugler, c.1951. (British Crown Copyright/M.O.D.)

An A.P.L. Sergeant Weapons Instructor (R.A.F.) pointing out the finer skills of the .303 Mk II Bren Gun to a *Jundi*, 1950s. The sergeant wears a bush hat with left-hand brim turned up. A locally-manufactured crossed *jambia* badge is pinned onto a green A.P.L. flash with vertical white line. (British Crown Copyright/M.O.D.)

A.P.L. Arab officer, 1950s. The all-khaki uniform bears a green lanyard and garter flashes. The R.A.F.-style rank insignia is green and white. The headdress reflects the Indian influence. The *mashedda* is khaki, and has a *khulla* on top. On the left-hand side is a green flash with white horizontal bar. (British Crown Copyright/M.O.D.)

Profile of an A.P.L. Arab officer showing parade uniform, 1950s. (British Crown Copyright/ M.O.D.)

soldier. The informality of the uniform "up-country" helped identify British personnel as belonging to the A.P.L. rather than to the British Army.

Ceremonial dress was worn by members of the Camel Troop, Camp Police and the Guard of Honour. This uniform consisted of a khaki or white drill bush jacket and shorts, black boots, and short puttees with green hosetops and green and white garter tabs. An elaborate Punjabi style white turban or *pagri*, with a *shamla*, was worn with a red stripe on the front, and a green flash with the A.P.L. badge on the left hand side. A khaki turban or *pagri* was the normal parade headdress. During the 1950s the British instructors wore a slouch hat with an A.P.L. flash of green white green, superimposed on which was a locally-made cap badge of metal crossed *jambias*. Officers wore a British officers' service dress cap. R.A.F. personnel were issued with the R.A.F. blue beret on which they wore the unofficial A.P.L. badge. Army personnel, who replaced the R.A.F. in 1957, sometimes wore an A.P.L. side hat, British army-style, of green with white piping.

Queen Elizabeth II authorised the badge of the A.P.L. on 11 December 1955. Its description is "Two *jambias* points downwards in saltire enfiled by a circlet. Motto "Peace be with you" in Arabic. The significance of the *jambias* was that they are weapons carried by all tribesmen in Aden, and are unique to them. The circlet of the traditional green colour of the unit suggests unity of the various formations of levies. Locally-made badges were worn until about 1958, when the army introduced an official A.P.L. cap badge, initially in brass and white metal or silver and gilt for officers. This badge was similar to the previous badge except that it now had a scroll with A.P.L. and the whole surmounted by the crown of Queen Elizabeth. An anodised aluminium badge with the same design was later issued. Brass A.P.L. shoulder titles were worn, although some troops wore unofficial white-on-green cloth titles with the name of their unit spelled out in full. Coloured lanyards were worn as follows:

HQ – green and white twist; 1st Btn – gold; 2nd Btn – green; 3rd Btn – red; 4th Btn – Cambridge blue.

Aden Signal Company, Bombay Sappers and Miners

In September 1915 a Sub-Inspector with three operators and six linemen arrived from India tasked with providing communications for the Aden Moveable Column, in addition to the regimental signallers of the infantry units.

It was originally thought that communications were needed for two brigades, however a decision was made to downgrade the theatre of operations and Lahej was allowed to remain in the hands of the Turkish Army. On 26

March 1917 the detachment officially became the Aden Signal Company. The unit included a Brigade Signal Section, Divisional H.Q. Section with two heavy cable sections, Motorcycle Section, Artillery Section, and a Line of Communications Section. The following year a wireless detachment was added. After hostilities ceased the company was re-designated Aden Brigade Signal Section, and in 1922 became the Aden Signal Section. This Indian Signal Corps unit became a Royal Signals unit in 1927.

Aden Transport Company

An Aden Transport Company existed from 1923 to 1928.

Aden Troop

On 16 November 1855 a troop of irregular horse was sanctioned for Aden. The officer appointed to command the troop sailed from India on 20 April 1856, however the ship returned to India. Although thirteen horses and two ponies were indented for on 3 March 1857, the irregular horse never arrived. Instead, the officer volunteered his troop for the Persian War, after which it went to India to serve against the Mutineers.

A Colonel Merewether finally raised a troop of cavalry in Aden in 1867-8, and named it the Aden Levy. Recruitment for the troop was made in Baluchistan (India), with volunteers coming from the Poona Horse and the 1st and 2nd Scinde Horse. The Levy was regularised as the Aden Troop, a sub-unit of the Indian Army. Indian Army officers were seconded to the troop, and by 1875 the unit's furthest outpost was at Khormaksar, on the isthmus of sand which linked Aden to the mainland.

In 1881 the Kotaibi tribe from the Radfan mountains commenced exacting dues on the Hardaba route. This ancient, but illegal, form of revenue collection was dealt with in July 1884 when it was found necessary to support the Amir of Dhala with 50 sabres of Aden Troop and some sappers. Following the destruction of a few forts the Kotaibi quickly gave in. The following year the troop revisited the area to deter Turkish encroachment. This had little effect as in the summer of 1886 the Turks established themselves near Jalela and built a fortified post.

During 1900-01 Aden Troop participated in operations in Jubaland, and between 1902-04 acted as escort to the Anglo-Turkish Boundary Commission. A highlight of the troop's existence was the Imperial Visit to India in 1911, during which it provided the King's escort in Aden. The troop was lined up four-deep, with horses and camels mounted by bearded, khaki-clad troopers. In 1915, the troop formed the advance guard during the British march to Lahej, a move aimed at preventing a Turkish advance upon Aden. The troop was disbanded in 1927, but a number of the troopers were later to see service with the newly-formed Aden Protectorate Levies and the Aden Armed Police.

During the sixty years of its existence the uniform of the Aden Troop would have undergone numerous changes, although information on dress is sketchy at best. In his book *Forces of the British Empire 1914* Nevins indicates that the uniform included a khaki turban, *kurta*, cummerbund, and breeches with khaki puttees. Indian Army ranks were used. The parade dress at the time of the Imperial visit was typical of an Indian cavalry regiment.

Desert Guards
Haras al Sahara

Desert Guards were auxiliaries of the Hadhrami Bedouin Legion and consisted of local tribesmen who were attached to H.B.L. posts. The tribesmen found their own weapons and rations, and were paid a monthly wage. Although ammunition was provided, they were expected to account for it. Some attempts were made to drill the tribesmen, although their principal value lay in their contacts with, and intelligence gathered from, local tribes. Nevertheless, they did take part in many desert skirmishes. Where supplied uniforms consisted of H.B.L. khaki *qamees* and a green chequered *imama* with black *aqu'al*.

Federal National Guard
Haras al Ittihad

With the creation of the Federation of the Amirates of the South in 1959, the Government Guards and Tribal Guard were renamed the Federal National Guard (F.N.G.). They became known as F.N.G.1 and F.N.G.2 respectively, and were placed under federal control. The new force continued to operate in the former Western Aden Protectorate as an armed gendarmerie, serving in lieu of a police force.

F.N.G.1 was recruited from all the states of the federation, and was directly controlled from the Federal National Guard Headquarters at Champion Lines in Aden. By contrast, F.N.G.2 consisted of former Tribal Guard or state forces, recruited entirely from within their own states. F.N.G.2 units were chiefly officered by relations and friends of the various state rulers. Although F.N.G.2 contingents were administered from F.N.G. Headquarters, in practice they conformed to the wishes of the State Rulers in most matters. The Commander

Brigadier J.H. Mallard, last commandant of the F.N.G. (Brig. Mallard)

F.N.G. never managed to get F.N.G.2 solely under his control because the state rulers, who collectively formed the Federal Council, always objected to loosing personal control of their own forces.

Unlike the Federal Regular Army (F.R.A.) the F.N.G. received no support or advice from the British army. Although the F.N.G. commander was British, almost all of the officers were Arab. One consequence of the different organisational structures was the considerable rivalry between the two forces. As the insurgency problem in the federation increased, so too did the pressure on the F.N.G.. There was general dissatisfaction on the British side regarding the F.N.G.'s standard and performance.

During the summer of 1965 a reorganisation of the F.N.G. took place, which included retraining and re-equipping thus rendering it better able to play a part in responding to the insurgency problem. F.N.G.1 was reorganised into four *katibas*, which were similar to infantry battalions. A committee was formed to advise on the future pattern of the federal Forces, and it was decided that the four *katibas* of F.N.G.1 should be absorbed into the F.R.A. to form the South Arabian Army (S.A.A.), while F.N.G. 2 should be expanded and joined to the existing Aden Police to form the new South Arabian Police (S.A.P.). During this period, the Federal Government was informed by H.M. Government that all British forces were to be pulled out of Aden, and that British military support to the Federal forces would cease. This reduced the authority of the State Rulers and the Federal Council. The two terrorist organisations, National Liberation Front (N.L.F.) and the Front for the Liberation of the South Yemen (F.L.O.S.Y.) were greatly encouraged, and were able to step up their operations against the Federal Government to a considerable degree. The Federal forces came under great political pressure to support the terrorist organisations. While still being paid by the federation, many members were secretly establishing links with the N.L.F., which soon established itself as the dominant terrorist force.

In 1967, the four *katibas* of F.N.G.1 joined the F.R.A. to form the South Arabian Army, but before the expansion and reorganisation of the new South Arabian police could be completed the final storm broke. Terrorist pressure intensified and revolutions took place in one state after another. In the last few months of the Federation, all of the state rulers disappeared over the border, the Federal Council ceased to operate, and the Minister of Internal Security left the country. As most of the officers of F.N.G. 2 were closely connected to the

F.N.G. bugler. Note the black headdress with tail hanging at rear. (Bill Cranston)

state rulers, most of them fled as well, thereby rendering adequate control of F.N.G.2 impossible.

Working dress for the Federal National Guard consisted of a khaki shirt, shorts, black hose tops with khaki puttees and boots. On occasion, khaki or green overalls were also worn by other ranks. Three types of headdress were worn. Officers wore a black *sedara*, or field service cap, with a green crown and green piping, on the front of which was placed a small-sized white metal F.N.G. cap badge. Other ranks were issued with a khaki beret, or a black turban, on both of which were worn brass badges. The ceremonial turbans had a black tail which hung down below the back of the neck. Black buttons, which bore the F.N.G. insignia, were worn by all ranks, and came in two sizes. A black lanyard was worn on the left shoulder. Officers wore green cloth Arabic shoulder titles sewn to the tops of their tunic sleeves, and highly decorated, locally-made, black cartridge belts together with a black Sam Browne belt. Arabic white metal shoulder titles were worn on some orders of dress, whilst those for other ranks were sometimes brass. Green cummerbunds were worn on ceremonial occasions.

Embellishments on the other ranks' khaki cloth tunic included khaki cloth shoulder titles with black Arabic script. Other ranks leather equipment consisted of black belts, ammunition pouches, and straps. British rank insignia was worn by all ranks.

Cap badges were made in white metal for officers and brass for other ranks. The Arabic motto on the cap badge translates as "God commands justice, the doing of good". Other insignia included khaki drill square patches with black numbers ranging from 1 to 24. Patterns for these patches were sealed on 7 November 1960. Tribal insignia was also authorised, and consisted of a khaki square with the name of the state in black Arabic lettering. Patterns for the tribal insignia, which was almost certainly used by F.N.G.2, were sealed on 10 February 1961. Black and silver buttons were issued, both of which bore the design of the cap badge. Small white metal collar badges, in mirrored pairs, were produced for officers.

Federal Regular Army

Jaish al Ittihad al Nidhami

The A.P.L. had formed part of the Imperial forces, but once handed over to the Federal Government as the Federal Regular Army (F.R.A.) on 30 November 1961, it owed allegiance to Aden, not London. The General Officer Commanding Middle East Land Forces (M.E.L.F.) continued to have some residual responsibilities for the F.R.A. until 1 April 1964 after which date the Federal Government had complete control. At the end of 1961 the strength of the F.R.A. was about 4,500 officers and men including about 400 seconded British personnel.

When formed, the F.R.A. consisted of: four infantry battalions, training battalion, armoured car squadron, signal squadron, motor transport company, supply platoon and force workshop. A British artillery battery supported the force. A fifth battalion was raised in 1964. Each battalion comprised three rifle companies, and a headquarters company containing a Vickers Medium Machine Gun platoon and a 3" mortar platoon. The training battalion was virtually a depot, and also administered the ceremonial camel troop, which was 16 camels strong and was all that was remained of the old A.P.L. Camel Company. Other sub-units included the apprentices' school and force band, which were included in the depot's strength.

F.R.A. Headquarters were at Seedaseer Lines, so named after the first battle honour of a battalion of the Mahratta Light Infantry, an Indian Regiment which had been sent to reinforce Aden's garrison on the outbreak of World War Two, and which was quartered in Khormaksar. The A.P.L. had taken over

Members of the F.R.A. man a 106mm anti-tank gun whilst observed by officers and local dignitaries. Photo taken during the 1960s. (John Daymond)

Lt. Col. Sandy Thomas, F.R.A., drives the leading Landrover whilst conducting Arab dignitaries through his area. (John Daymond)

Photo of a member of the F.R.A. ceremonial camel section, from a recruiting poster. The lance carries a dark green above white pennant. Headdress is dark green, as is cummerbund, worn over a white tunic. A brown leather 1903 cavalry pattern bandoleer is strapped over the left shoulder. Dark green hosetops and khaki puttees are worn with black boots. (Bill Cranston)

the lines as a headquarters after the end of the war, which consequently became the headquarters of the F.R.A..

During its short existence, the F.R.A. continued the traditions of the A.P.L. and became a very professional military force. It continued to serve throughout the former Western Aden Protectorate, which was now known as the Federation of South Arabia since the Eastern Aden Protectorate never joined the Federation. Tactics and armament remained similar to that of the A.P.L., although more emphasis was placed on motor transport and armoured cars. A major action with Arab dissidents in the Radfan Mountains was eventually contained due to increased assistance from British regiments. The main frontier garrisons were at Dhala, Mukheiras and Beihan. Arab nationalism was increasing throughout the area, and increased pressure from Egypt and the Yemen ensured that trouble was constantly "brewing" throughout the Federation. Following Britain's declaration to quit South Arabia, it appeared inevitable that the Federation would collapse and civil war would ensue. In an effort to unify the various armed forces in the country it was decided to form the South Arabian Army (S.A.A.), which would be based on an amalgamation of the Federal Regular Army and its old rival the Federal National Guard. It was also planned that the Hadhrami Bedouin Legion would also come into this grouping. On 1 June 1967 the F.R.A. was re-designated as the South Arabian Army.

When "up-country" the uniform of the F.R.A. was similar to that of the A.P.L., consisting of a khaki drill shirt and shorts, rolled-down socks, brown plimsolls and a smart, small, Audhali khaki head cloth. The white *mashedda* of the A.P.L. was replaced by one of dark green for ceremonial purposes. Unlike the A.P.L., the F.R.A. was issued with Arabic rank insignia, so that the pips were replaced with stars, and the crown with stars and crescents. F.R.A. forces had their own cap badge, which was similar to the old A.P.L. badge save that the crown was replaced by a star and crescent, and the scroll was in Arabic. An Arabic anodised aluminium shoulder title was worn along with anodised buttons, which featured the cap badge design. Officer's quality silver and gilt cap and collar badges were also produced and worn.

Government Guards

Haras al Hakooma

The Government Guards were a formation whose existence was conceived by Major Basil W. Seager C.M.G., O.B.E., who was 1st Political Officer in 1937. He suggested to the government that a frontier force of approximately 100 men should be formed. By March 1938 approval had been received to raise the Government Guards. It was intended that the force would also be used within the Protectorate limits, in areas adjacent to the Yemen frontier where there were likely to be inter-tribal disputes between tribes living on either side of the border. It was decided that the force should also be available for internal security work.

Captain R.A.B. Hamilton (later Lord Belhaven and Stenton) became the first commander. A headquarters was constructed in one of the numerous date gardens at Sheikh Othman, just outside Aden. After a year it was planned to double the strength of the Government Guards, and to include a troop of horse. The irregular nature of the Government Guard is nicely put by Lord Belhaven and Stenton in his book *The Uneven Road*. He described the men as being older and more seasoned to the mischances of the world than the men of the Levies – men of standing in their own tribe, with their own characteristics which no parade discipline could suppress. The Guards were unofficially known as "Ham's Outfit" or "Ham's catch-em-aliveos".

The Government Guards – a gendarmerie paid for by H.M. Government – were deployed about the Western Aden Protectorate. They were to be found along the frontier in a number of small forts and provided escorts and static guards. On occasion, they were able to provide support to various tribal guards. Because of their wide deployment, and the police function which they had to perform, they had less opportunity for formal training as soldiers. Consequently, the Guards were less technically competent than the Aden Protectorate Levies, although their respective purpose and organisation were quite different. More lightly-armed than the Levies, the Guards possessed Jordan-trained Arab officers who were promoted to appointments formerly held by British officers. The "Arabisation" of the Guards created a different military environment to that of the Levies, who were based on British regular infantry lines. This became a problem in later years as the Levies regarded themselves as a more professional force.

In 1938 Government Guards were given the additional task of guarding vital points, with prime responsibility for the Aden pipeline and water supply. Patrol duties included a car patrol, which consisted of 1 *Rais* (captain) and 6 *Askaris* (soldiers). Every two hours 2 men were to patrol in the car from Government Guards Garden (headquarters) at Sheikh Othman to the Isthmus parapets. A camel patrol, consisting of a *Rais* and 6 *Askaris*, patrolled every two hours from the Levy fence via Government Guards' Headquarters to Bir Fadhl. A post of 3 men was stationed at Khormaksar Bridge, where the water pipe emerged to the surface of the ground. A further six posts were located at the wells of the Government Guards' Garden. Each post consisted of 3 men.

From 1940 until the Italian surrender in East Africa "Ham's Outfit" also contained a "naval" element. This consisted of the crews of four small *dhows* fitted with auxiliary engines. These were used to harry the small Italian-occupied ports on the Somali coast and to blockade the Straits of Bab al Mandeb. They mounted two-pounder guns and with a lucky shot one succeeded in sinking a German cargo ship trying to escape from the Red Sea by night. The naval commander in Aden refused to acknowledge these vessels as coming under his command, describing them as a bunch of pirates, and would not allow them to fly the naval ensign. Consequently the flotilla commander, an Irishman, flew the Cross of St. Patrick.

Fort Thumier guarding the Aden road, Radfan, Western Aden Protectorate, February 1958. Two Government Guards officers walk hand-in-hand, an acceptable and normal sign of friendship among Arab soldiers. The fort was built to protect travellers from being robbed by the self-styled "Wolves of the Jebal Radfan". (Major C. Butt)

By the early 1950s the strength of the Guards had reached over 500 men, who were dispersed in numerous posts throughout the Western Aden Protectorate. Headquarters moved to a small reserve at Khormaksar in Aden Colony, and the unit was commanded by a British Commandant, 4 British, and 14 Arab officers. Depending on the terrain, the soldiers travelled either on foot, camel or lorry. Recruitment was from all tribes in the Western Aden Protectorate, no segregation occurring. Many of the permanent posts were in some of the most inaccessible parts of the Protectorate, but contact was maintained by means of wireless telegraphy.

In 1959, with the creation of the Amirates of the South, the Government Guards and Tribal Guard merged. The new force was titled the Federal National Guard.

The original uniform of the Government Guard was the war dress of the Mushreq tribes (eastern tribes from Awaliq and Wahidi). This consisted of a loin cloth, head cloth, and plaid of indigo blue, with a dagger and a cartridge belt. A blue bush shirt was also worn. For desert work all of this was covered with a khaki head cloth and smock. Boots were not worn. Later the Guards wore distinctive uniforms consisting of khaki shorts and shirt, a leather belt superimposed on a khaki cummerbund, puttees and sandals of local

Government Guard fort at Merta, Western Aden Protectorate, May 1958. The fort was located about 2,000 yards from the Yemeni military border town of Am Soumah. The Landrover and crew are A.P.L. This fort featured in a number of border incidents. (Major C. Butt)

manufacture. Headdress consisted of a black turban with a green flash on the left hand side, superimposed on which was the crossed rifles cap badge.

By the late 1950s parade dress was modified to include black boots and black leather equipment and ammunition carriers, which carried loose ammunition rather than clips. A black belt was worn over a dark green cummerbund. The black turban was retained, and included the green flash on the left-hand side with a blackened Government Guard cap badge. In the field, a khaki *mashedda* or large khaki beret (soup-plate style) was worn. Officers'-quality cap badges were of blackened brass or bronze, while other ranks cap badges were of cast brass and came without a crown. Buttons were black, and bore the king's crown and G.G. on them. The back was stamped "FIRMIN LONDON". A skill-at-arms badge, "Marksman", consisted of crossed rifles, embroidered in black mercerised cotton on khaki drill. This was sealed by Crown Agents on 24 September 1957. A khaki cloth shoulder title, with GOVERNMENT GUARDs written in black Arabic script was worn at the top of the sleeve or a brass G.G. title. Weapons used were the .303 Rifle SMLE No.1 Mk III and Bren Gun.

Hadhrami Bedouin Legion
Jaish al Badiyah al Hadramiyah

Modelled on the successful Arab Legion, the Hadhrami Bedouin Legion (H.B.L.) was formed in 1940 as a British military force to be used in the Eastern Aden Protectorate. The H.B.L. was an all-Arab regiment, paid for by Britain and used as the Resident Adviser's own force until 1956, after which a British officer commanded the force. Bedouin tribesmen were recruited to form a light infantry that was tough and highly mobile in difficult terrain.

In 1936 Harold Ingrams was appointed Resident Adviser to the Hadhramaut States and British Agent, Eastern Aden Protectorate. His main concern was to end the endemic tribal warfare. By using the successful establishment of the Arab Legion as his model, Ingrams was able to produce a similar force. In 1939, 3 Jordanian officers on secondment from the Arab Legion arrived in the Hadhramaut, and the first 50 tribesmen were recruited and trained at the H.B.L. Liejun post at Gheil bin Yumain in Hamumi tribal territory. The fort was built in similar fashion to the desert posts of Glubb

Government Guards at Merta Fort, Western Aden Protectorate, June 1958. Two are in full uniform, i.e. black equipment, dark green cummerbund, black *mashedda* with green flash, and G.G. cap badge. They are armed with SMLE No.1 Mk.III rifles. Note ammunition carriers in place of British army pouches. Two other soldiers are in working dress, and wear khaki berets with G.G. badge on a green flash. Their locally-made ammunition belts are for carrying separate cartridges rather than clips. (Major C. Butt)

Pasha's Arab Legion in Trans-Jordan. A wireless station was installed to provide communications with Mukalla, but the remoteness was a disadvantage, headquarters consequently moving to Dis, near Mukalla. Leijun became an outpost, and as men became available, further outposts were manned at Bir Asakir and Al Abr. Many of the forts had a "Beau Geste" appearance.

Rais Barakat was the first commandant, and his second-in-command was Khalid. In about 1947 these two officers were recalled to Jordan and Abdul Hadi Hammad took command. Later, a more senior Arab Legion officer, Qaid Naif al Faiz, was brought in to take command. During the famine years of 1944 and 1948, the H.B.L. was used for the distribution of famine relief supplies. H.B.L. schools were built for both boys and girls, and famine orphans were given the chance to gain an education. Many of the students went on to become wireless operators, clerks and mechanics in the force.

In 1950 three more forts were built at Zamakh, Minwakh, and Markaz Hajr. The strength of the H.B.L. was now about 170, and doubled within the next two of years. Thamud Well was occupied in 1953, Sanau in 1954, and Habarut, on the Omani border, in 1956. Naif returned to Jordan in 1955, and was replaced by Khalaf Qaftan, but he too was recalled in 1957. Jock Snell of the Sussex Regiment became commandant for a short period, after which a South African, Pat Gray, took command. He reorganized the H.B.L. into what amounted to infantry-sized companies, with each company being assigned an area of responsibility for six months before either moving on to another area, or into reserve at Headquarters. Qu'aiti forces were left to maintain peace and order in the settled areas of the state, including the north-west plateau whilst the H.B.L. were used to back-up the states and the huge area of desert and mountain beyond. Heavier weapons were introduced, and four Ferret armoured cars were acquired in 1960. At the time that the Federation was being formed the eastern states had already combined their forces against mutual danger, and saw little advantage in joining what they looked upon as a gaggle of small districts whose administrations had a long way to go before they reached the condition of the Qu'aitis and Kathiris.

The eastern Sultanate of Mahra was technically a part of the Eastern Aden Protectorate, and had its Sultan on Socotra Island, many miles from the state proper. In reality Mahra was an enormous area which had seen very few Europeans. Although a treaty had been signed with the Sultan, he did not speak for all of the people, and the state was a lawless area into which few outsiders dared to venture. Oil exploration was the incentive required to establish a British presence in the area. In the early 1960s, a force of the H.B.L. managed to establish a company-strength fort at Al Gheidha, the capital of Mahra. Another fort was built at Marait, and a small state force was also raised. Major David Eales,

Boys from the military school in Mukalla parade at the Sultan's palace, c.1960. The headdress is a white *imama* with black *aqu'al*. A dark blue *qamees* is worn with red sash and cummerbund. (Mrs Edith Gray)

H.B.L. scout cars, c.1960. (Mrs Snell)

second-in-command, was murdered at Marait by a Hamumi *jundi* who held a grudge against him – the murderer escaped. The following year Pat Gray, the Commandant, was ambushed and died of his wounds. Colonel Eric Johnson, Military Adviser to the Resident Adviser, took over command with Wakil Qaid Salim Umar al Johi as second-in-command. The force remained loyal to its paymasters, and in 1967 mounted a successful operation utilising R.A.F. Beverley aircraft to flush out all National Liberation Front (N.L.F.) supporters on Socotra Island. With great flair the H.B.L. captured the entire Mahra N.L.F. hierarchy. After the British left Aden the H.B.L., and other local forces were, with varying degrees of success, absorbed into the People's Democratic Republic of Yemen armed forces.

A light brown, calf-length *qamees*, or outer shirt, of khaki drill (Crown Agents SD2) was the original H.B.L. uniform, while parade dress was white. In about 1958 the *qamees* was superceded by a khaki shirt and shorts, however the white *qamees* was retained as dress for parades. Soldiers wore a red canvas cummerbund, which had a sash on the left-hand side. Over the cummerbund was worn an H.B.L. leather ammunition belt, which had a flat brass buckle bearing the H.B.L. inscription. Headdress consisted of a red check *imama* (*kufiya*), which was similar to the headdress of the Arab Legion. The *imama* was held in place by a black goat's hair *aqu'al*. This is a camel hobble, which is tied in between a camel's forefeet with two strings, these hanging down the back when the *aqu'al* is worn on a man's head. Footwear was not issued until 1954, when a contingent was sent to Aden for the Queen's Visit. Sandals, of the type issued to the Government Guards, were issued to the contingent to protect their feet from Aden's tarred roads. Footwear was again issued in 1960, when the H.B.L. and M.R.A. were involved in suppression of a tribal war. In the field, officers usually wore much the same uniform as the men, but when in Mukalla, long trousers, tunic, and brown shoes were often worn and on suitable occasions, a highly polished Sam Browne. Revolvers were not generally used, as the rifle was considered the mark of a man.

The design of the brass headdress badge, worn on the *aqu'al*, was a wreath with two crossed *jambias*, points uppermost, and a scroll with the inscription JAISH AL BADIYAH AL HADHRAMIYAH (Hadhrami Bedouin Legion) in Arabic script. This badge was later superseded by a locally-made white metal badge, bearing the inscription JAISH AL BADIYAH (Bedouin Legion) in Arabic script. Brass (and later white metal) shoulder titles were designed by Qu'aiti Sultan Saleh bin Ghalib, whose hobbies included calligraphy. A red piece of cloth was worn under the shoulder title. When Colonel Gray reorganised the Legion he introduced single colour underlays for each rifle company, blue and white for signals, and red and blue for transport. Photographic

Typical H.B.L. fort in the Eastern Aden Protectorate. A red and white H.B.L. flag is flying, bearing the legion's insignia in its centre. (Mrs Edith Gray)

H.B.L. officers take a break, c.1960. The intricate, locally-made, soft leather equipment can be seen clearly. Red H.B.L. lanyards are worn. This rifle company has a black underlay beneath its shoulder title. (Mrs Edith Gray)

H.B.L. lorried infantry "up country", c.1960. The soldiers in this section are carrying Rifles No.4 Mk.I. (Mrs Edith Gray)

H.B.L. convoy in the interior, c.1960. All vehicles carry a red band over their bonnet, whilst the RL Bedford 3-ton lorries also have white roofs enabling easy identification from the air. (Mrs Edith Gray)

evidence shows that the rifle company colours included red, black, gold/ yellow, blue and green. Officers wore a red lanyard on the left shoulder.

Photographic evidence from the early 1960s shows that H.B.L. vehicles were marked with a red line across the bonnet as an aid in identification, particularly by air, and a white H.B.L. badge was painted on vehicle doors. R.L. Bedford lorries had the cab roof painted white. Red tactical sign plates were placed at the front and back of vehicles. These had a white Arabic inscription stating Hadhrami Bedouin Legion. Later that decade the vehicles reverted to a more sombre British army green. A yellow-over-red tactical sign, identical to the British Armoured Corps, was later used.

Rifles issued to the H.B.L. were originally Indian-made .303 SMLE No.1 Mk III's, which were later replaced by the Rifle No.4 Mk I. As with other Eastern Aden Protectorate forces, captured Italian weapons were used shortly after the end of the Second World War. These consisted of Italian Breda 6.5 mm LMGs and Austrian Schwarzlose 8mm MMGs. Ammunition and belts were no longer available after 1952, and they were replaced by .303 Bren Guns.

Imad Levy

Imad was an Arab village a few miles along the coast east of Aden. In December 1915 a small levy of 100 men was raised to protect the village and to provide intelligence and guides for the British forces fighting in the Aden hinterland. The levy was officered by British and Indian soldiers.

In his "Report on the Operations of the Aden Field Force of 1st April – 18th August 1917" the G.O.C. Aden states that on 9 April 1917 cavalry and infantry scouts sniped Jabir in the morning. In the afternoon some Somalis at Jabir attempted a reprisal on Imadis cutting wood in "no man's land". Their attack was repulsed by the Imad Levy.

The Imad Levy grew in size and was later known as the Arab Levy.

Kathiri Armed Constabulary

Shurtah al Masaliha al Kathiriyah

The Kathiri Sultans were descended from Badr Abu Tuwairiq, who led the Kathiri tribe from the High Yemen into the Hadhramaut during the latter part of the 15th Century. They proceeded to overrun the area and ruled after the fashion of the times. They built up a tribal confederation known as the Shanafir around them. To support their rule they employed mercenary Yafa'is soldiers from the mountains of north-east Aden. In the latter part of the 16th Century a group of those mercenaries, led by members of the small Qu'aiti sub-tribe, seized the area of Al Qatn, which had the best agricultural land in the Hadhramaut, and established their own rule there. Consequently, a series of wars between the Kathiris and the Qu'aitis ensued, and over the next three hundred years most towns changed hands at least twice. Many Hadhramis travelled abroad to India and the Far East to trade or to serve as mercenary soldiers. About 1840 the two most successful Arab mercenary soldiers in India were Umar Bin Awadh al Qu'aiti and Ghalib bin Mohsin al Kathiri, who each commanded a regiment in the army of the Nizam of Hyderabad. At feud in Hadhramaut, they continued the feud in Hyderabad, to the annoyance and disquiet of the Nizam. As the Qu'aiti had been in India longer, and had acquired more friends at court, the Kathiri was obliged to depart, and went home to make life difficult for the Qu'aiti in Hadhramaut.

By 1880, Kathiri State had lost much of its territory to Qu'aiti after a series of disastrous wars. The Kathiri Sultan found his African slaves more reliable administrators than his fellow tribesmen so that the descendants of the Sultan's slave army formed the majority of a force of about 80 tribal guard in 1939. Harold Ingrams had proposed the force several years earlier, and Captain R.A.B. Hamilton was tasked with raising the Kathiri Armed Constabulary (K.A.C.) funded by a British government subsidy and the Kathiri State. Britain also supplied rifles and ammunition. The force was inspected by a British officer and trained by Arab instructors, and gradually the African element was replaced by tribesmen.

During the Bin Abdat crises of the 1940s the K.A.C. was too small in numbers to cope with the opposition, and support had to be brought in from Qu'aiti and Hyderabad to deal with the problem. After the crisis was resolved the K.A.C. maintained a fair degree of peace and quiet via small outposts and a reserve at Husn Howarith, on the eastern outskirts of Seiyun. Within the confines of a small state, and possessing a good commander, Saleh al Jabri – an N.C.O. transferred from the H.B.L. and commissioned – the Kathiri State became a fairly peaceful place until independence.

The Kathiri were originally armed with the French Le Gras rifle, known in the Hadhramaut as *Hotfa*. These used lead bullets and black powder cartridges. They were replaced by Italian 6.5 mm rifles and Austrian 8mm cavalry carbines captured in Eritrea during the Second World War. During the 1950s these weapons were replaced with British .303 Rifles, SMLE No.1 Mk III, manufactured in India during the Second World War.

The K.A.C. wore a khaki drill shirt and shorts, with a brown leather belt. K.A.C. headdress consisted of a blue-and-white chequed *imama* with black *aqu'al*. No cap badge was ever made, but the constabulary used a straight metal shoulder title with Arabic script. Boots were not worn.

Aden Police band perform at the police barracks in Crater, 1965. Their red *pagri* and *shamla* have a blue *khulla*. (F.W. Bird)

A.P.L. Ferret armoured car, c.1959. Note the badge painted on its side. (David Birtles)

Three young H.B.L. *jundies* smartly turned out, c.1960. Note the black leather belt with brass buckle. They have a yellow-over-red underlay attached to their shoulder titles. (Mrs Edith Gray)

A.P.L. Camel Troop at Seedaseer Lines, c.1959. (Major C.A. Stahelin)

Ataq Airstrip, with F.N.G. officers and men in the foreground, c.1961. Note the sergeant wearing green overalls and a cotton bandoleer around his waist. (Jim Ellis)

A.P.L. Ceremonial Guard marching with bayonets fixed on Rifles No.4 Mk. I, c.1959. The red stripe on the turban denotes membership of the Ceremonial Guard. (Major C.A. Stahelin)

F.R.A. Ceremonial Camel Troop (Major A.H. Fraser)

F.R.A. mortar section. The mortar is a British Ordnance 3″ with Mk V barrel, No.6 baseplate, Mk V bipod and utilises the Mk II sight. The bombs are probably H.E. rounds, identifiable by the flat round 162 fuse. Rifles No.4 Mk I are being carried. (Major C.A. Stahelin)

Sultan Saleh bin Jabal al Audhali, Federal Minister of Security, visiting an F.N.G. outpost during the early 1960s. Behind him flies the flag of the Federation. (Jim Ellis).

F.N.G. fort at Dhala, early 1960s. (Jim Ellis)

F.N.G. officer Qaid Fadhl Abdullah relaxes with troops, c.1961. Note the variety of locally-made leather equipment being worn. (Jim Ellis)

F.N.G. officers, Sharif Haider in centre, c.1961. Note the *sedara* hat with silver F.N.G. hat badge in the front. (Jim Ellis)

Officers outside the British Residency, Mukalla, early 1960s. Left to right:- Rais Saleh bin Salaan, K.A.C.; Rais Yusaf al Kathiri, H.B.L.; Rais Shaikh Azzani, H.B.L. Signals; Sheikh Amin, Kathiri State Secretary. (Jim Ellis)

Hadhrami Bedouin Legion barracks, situated on the outskirts of Mukalla, c.1960. The city was the capital of Qu'aiti State in the Hadhramaut and the largest in the Eastern Aden Protectorate. The soldiers stand beside the H.B.L. monument, bearing the Legion's badge painted onto it. Flanking either side of it are Austrian Schwarzlose machine guns, which were acquired following the Italian surrender in Eritrea during the Second World War. They had originally belonged to the Austro-Hungarian army during the First World War, and had found their way into Italian service. Ammunition and belts had run out by 1952 and the weapons were replaced by .303 Bren guns. Behind the monument stands the Legion's flagpole. The buildings in the background are the Legion's administrative offices. (Mrs Edith Gray)

Three M.R.A. officers, c.1960. A Qu'aiti State award is worn by Captain Rubaiya, A.D.C. to the Sultan (centre left). All ranks wore British rank insignia. The officer to the right, *Wakil Qaid* (Major) Abdulwhabib Al Jahwary, deputy M.R.A. commander, wears an old King's Crown British major's rank on his shoulder strap. The M.R.A. wore khaki Indian-style turbans with *khulla* and *shamla*. (Mrs Edith Gray)

M.R.A. with red turbans giving "eyes right" whilst on parade at the British Residency in Mukalla, c.1960. A Mukalla Sultanate bandsman can be seen to the right of the picture. (Jim Ellis)

Senior military and police officers prepare to review a parade in the compound of the British Residency, Mukalla, E.A.P., c.1964. Left to right: O.C., H.B.L. Military School; O.C., Prison Service; O.C., Civil Police; C.O., Q.A.C.; C.O., M.R.A.; Commander Qu'aiti Forces, Saleh bin Someida. (Jim Ellis)

Qu'aiti Armed Constabulary being inspected at the British Residency, Mukalla, c.1964. They are wearing their khaki uniform, with khaki *imama* and black *aqu'al*. H.B.L. and M.R.A. troops parade to their right. (Jim Ellis)

Lahej Police
Shurtah Lahej

Lahej possessed its own police force, which included a traffic police section, and responsibility for the prison. Police uniform consisted of a khaki drill tunic and trousers, dark blue putties worn up to the knee and *chaplis*. The black leather belt that was worn had a large metal buckle similar in size to that of the Aden Police. The traffic police wore white sleeves. Lahej police were quite distinctive in that they had their own unique head-dress, which was a khaki pith helmet with cloth flap covering the neck. This style of helmet was very similar to that worn by police in Jordan, but without the spike on top. A metal hat badge was fixed in the front, which was of a similar shape and size to the Aden Police cap badge. Although unconfirmed, the badge is reputed to have borne the following inscription in Arabic: SULTANATE OF LAHEJ POLICE.

Lahej Policeman, 1963. The headdress is similar to a Jordanian Police helmet, but without a spike. A Sultanate of Lahej Police cap badge is worn on its front. (Michael Crouch)

Lahej Trained Forces
Ku'aat Lahej

Lahej was the largest city in the Western Aden Protectorate, and in many respects mirrored Mukalla in the Eastern Aden Protectorate as the pre-eminent seat of control for that area. A British Political Officer resided there, but Lahej never possessed the same importance, from a colonial perspective, as Mukalla did.

By the late 1930s the Lahej Trained Forces (L.T.F.) wore a uniform of khaki shirt, shorts and *pagri*. No specific headdress badge was ever produced. By the 1950s the L.T.F. was being called the Lahej Regular Army (L.R.A.). In 1952 the

L.R.A. is reported to have included a mounted section for escort duties, brass band and at least 4 pieces of artillery, in addition to its infantry component. Following a visit to Scotland the Sultan introduced a pipe band, which became highly sought-after in Aden for functions. In 1957 the entire band accompanied the Sultan and most of the L.R.A. into Yemen to escape internal feuding within the state. The military was rebuilt as the Lahej Tribal Guards by Ali bin Ahmed, a nephew of the succeeding Sultan, Fadhl bin Ali.

Mahra Tribal Guard
Haras al Qabila al Mahra

Mahra was the last state in the Protectorates to be pacified. Located in the east of the Eastern Aden Protectorate, Mahra was a lawless tract of land remote from civilisation. A treaty had been signed with the Sultan, who resided on the island of Socotra. In theory the state was a part of the Eastern Aden Protectorate. In reality it contained many tribes who refused to accept the Sultan's authority. For example, there were Kathiri tribesmen who had been feuding with the Mahra for almost four centuries! Consequently, the treaty with the British was a worthless piece of paper. The British turned a blind eye to the problem as it was not worth the cost of a major expedition until oil companies showed an interest in the area.

It was not until the early 1960s that the Hadhrami Bedouin Legion were called upon to show a presence in the state and establish a number of small forts there. This was done with some skill and daring, and, as a consequence, a small Mahra Tribal Guard (M.T.G.) was established in 1965. This was similar in structure to the former Tribal Guards of the Western Aden Protectorate, who had been merged with the Government Guard into F.N.G.2 in 1959. The Mahra were never considered for membership of the Federation. The Colonial Office subsidised the Mahra State, and the bulk of the Mahra Tribal Guard's money came from that subsidy. Little is known of the unit, other than that the soldiers were uniformed in the usual khaki drill shirt and shorts, and had the distinction of wearing a black and white *imama* headdress with *aqu'al*.

Military Assistant To The Resident Adviser, Eastern Aden Protectorate
Masa'ad al Mustashar al Harbi

Unlike the Western Aden Protectorate, which was close to Aden Colony and consequently to support from political and military forces, the Eastern Aden

Protectorate was remote and difficult to reach, except by air. The eastern states also had to be aware of the ever-present threat from Saudi Arabia. Nevertheless, most of its difficulties were internal. Harold Ingrams, the first Resident Adviser, recognised the unique difficulties of his domain. Accordingly, he established the post of Military Assistant to the Resident Adviser (M.A.R.A.), aimed at raising the standard of training of the various military and paramilitary forces of the protectorate, in particular of the newly-raised Hadhrami Bedouin Legion. A number of very experienced and capable officers served in this post until 1967.

The Military Assistant was tasked with ensuring that all of the various military forces in the Eastern Aden Protectorate received sufficient training, and that these units were up to the standards required. Because of his close liaison with the different military groups it was only natural that he was able to co-ordinate the movement of all of the forces in that protectorate. He had a well-trained and disciplined – albeit somewhat diverse – force at his disposal, which was attuned to the needs of every corner of the protectorate except Mahra State, which was not pacified until the 1960s. The combination of stable military force, good colonial administration, fewer sheikhdoms and sultanates, and its geographical location, meant that the Eastern Aden Protectorate was more peaceful and more autonomous than the Western Aden Protectorate. This was reflected in the fact that none of the eastern states (with the exception of Wahidi) were to join the Federation.

Mukalla Prison
Shurtah Li Sejun Bil Mukalla

In Qu'aiti State there were a number of Armed Constabulary lockups, but only one prison, which was situated in Mukalla. The prison was well-run and organised, but the accommodation is reported to have been basic. Prison police wore a curved brass shoulder title, which bore the Arabic inscription SHURTAH LI SEJUN BIL MUKALLA, which translates as Mukalla Prison Police. This title was first issued in 1964.

Mukalla Regular Army
Jaish al Mukalla al Nidhami

By far the largest and most developed state in the Eastern Aden Protectorate was the Qu'aiti Sultanate of Shihr and Mukalla. The Sultan who resided in the city of Mukalla was also hereditary commander of the bodyguard of the Nizam of Hyderabad, the largest native state in India. His estates in Hyderabad were lucrative and helped to shore up the shakier finances of his state in Arabia.

The Mukalla Regular Army (M.R.A.) existed for many years but the date of formation is unclear. However, the Qu'aiti Sultans had possessed soldiery of one sort or another, including Indians, since the mid-nineteenth century, when they waged a protracted but successful war with the Kathiris and others. An early mention of the army is to be found in *The Historical Record of the Imperial Visit to India 1911*, which records that the Sultan of "Shehr and Mokalla" was escorted by a body of horsemen in red and white uniforms.

During the 1930s the state possessed a trained military force of some 400 men, mainly Yafa'i tribesmen and the descendants of African slaves, plus about 1,000 or more irregular tribesmen. The officers were Indian, although they drilled in English. On ceremonial parades they wore blue and gold laced tunics, red breeches with a broad blue stripe, and squat *tarbooshes*. A small artillery section of two 2.75" mountain guns provided "firepower". They were known as "pip-squeaks", and were capable of blowing holes in most of the mud forts of up-country malcontents. These guns, which could be carried by camel and quickly assembled, lasted until 1955. They were then replaced by a 2 pdr anti-tank gun which could be towed by a Landrover. There were also a band and a bodyguard of lancers mounted on camels who wore a blue and red uniform. Only the band and infantry survived until 1967. While on active service, camels and often donkeys were hired for activities in country inaccessible to motor transport. Until the 1930s armament was mainly the Martini-Henry, a one-shot Snider-action weapon firing lead bullets of about 0.4 inches with black powder cartridges. These were later replaced by Indian-produced SMLE .303 rifles.

During 1938 Colonel Robinson of the A.P.L. spent some time with the M.R.A. and put them on a sound footing. After the Second World War further rearmament occurred using weapons captured from the Italians in Ethiopia, Eritrea and Somaliland. Breda 6.5mm light machine guns, and ex-Austrian 8mm carbines and Schwarzlose medium machine guns were available. The Austrian weapons had been captured by the Italians in 1918. After the ammunition ran out the M.R.A. were re-armed with No. 4 rifles and Brens.

A proportion of the force was always on duty in small groups in distant parts of the state, cooperating closely with the British-paid Hadhrami Bedouin Legion. The tactics of the two forces remained very similar. With independence the Yafa'i element drifted away, usually taking their arms with them. Many found their way to the Persian Gulf and enlisted in the forces of the Emirates. As long as Qaid Saleh bin Someida' commanded the M.R.A. they remained effective. However, in 1966 he was promoted to the command of all Qu'aiti

Sultan Ghalib of Mukalla with his A.D.C., 1960s. (Owain Raw-Rees)

M.R.A. on parade at the Sultan's palace. Officers wear khaki tunic, *pagri* with *shamla*, and shorts. Other ranks wear khaki uniforms with red *pagri* and cummerbund, the latter beneath a leather belt. (Jim Ellis)

forces. His successor, a Yafa'i named Qaid Ahmed al Yezidi, did not possess the same drive or charisma, and as a consequence the reliability of the M.R.A. became suspect. In 1967 this became rather obvious when an N.L.F.-inspired mob broke into the British Residency compound, forcing the H.B.L. to fire over their heads to disperse them. The M.R.A. guard in the Sultan's Palace opposite fired on the upper floors of the Residency until the Sultan personally intervened.

Following its abandonment by the British independence soon came to the Eastern Aden Protectorate. When the Qu'aiti and Kathiri Sultans were both in Geneva at the behest of the British and the United Nations the small British presence was withdrawn. Bin Someid'a and the Governor of Mukalla, Badr al Kasadi held the remains of the Qu'aiti administration together until over-whelmed by the National Liberation Front (N.L.F.), who imprisoned both along with others who opposed them. Whilst in prison, these two kept the spirits of the other prisoners up until an exasperated N.L.F. executed them.

During the Second World War the red and blue uniforms were discarded for khaki shirts and shorts with locally-made leather equipment. For ceremonial parades a red Indian-style turban replaced the work dress khaki turban, and a red cummerbund was worn under the brown leather belt. No footwear was worn. Whilst on garrison duty officers wore a British-style black field service hat with red piping, crown and peak. Other ranks had a plain khaki field service hat. On parade officers wore khaki Indian-style turbans with *shamla*, shirts, trousers, Sam Browne, sword and tan shoes. Whilst attached to the H.B.L. the gunners had the distinction of wearing the Hadhrami Bedouin Legion *imama* and *aqu'al*. The band, known as the Mukalla Sultanate Band, originally had a blue, red and yellow uniform, selected by the Sultan. This was later changed to a white turban, jacket and long trousers. The band was about 25 men strong.

The M.R.A. did not have its own cap badge but all ranks wore brass shoulder titles. Designed by Sultan bin Ghalib, these were worn from 1947. A band shoulder title was introduced in 1960. British rank insignia was worn by all E.A.P. forces.

The ranks within the Qu'aiti Armed Forces were as follows:

Musheer	Commander in Chief (The Sultan)
Liwa	Major General
Aqid	Colonel
Qaid	Lieutenant Colonel
Wakil Qaid	Major
Rais	Captain
Mulazim Awal	Lieutenant
Mulazim Thani	Second Lieutenant

The commanding officer, M.R.A., delivers a speech during the early 1960's. (Jim Ellis)

The Mukalla Sultanate Band, c.1964. They wear white *pagri*, white ceremonial dress and black shoes. They are followed by a company of M.R.A. distinguished by the rank and file's red *pagri*, which replaced those of khaki for ceremonial parades. (Jim Ellis)

Na'qib	Sergeant-Major
Na'ib	Sergeant (There was no Staff Sergeant rank)
Ar'rif	Corporal
Wakil Ar'rif	Lance Corporal
Jundi	Private
Jundi Murash'shah	Officer Cadet
Shabit	Cadet

Ordnance Depot, Aden

The Indian Army Service Corps maintained an ordnance depot in Aden from 1862 until 1947, when it was handed over to the Royal Army Service Corps.

Qu'aiti Armed Constabulary

Shurtah al Masaliha al Qu'aitiya

During the early twentieth century the Qu'aiti Sultain maintained a force of Yafa'i irregulars in the settled areas along the coast, and in those parts of the Hadhramaut which gave allegiance to him. The constabulary were housed in forts or fortified houses in or near towns and villages. They were paid a retainer, and allowed the privilege of private trade. Their duties included delivering summonses, supervising punishments and collecting fines and taxes. The soldiers were usually recruited from the mountains north east of Aden. In the early days the Qu'aiti Armed Constabulary were armed with the French Le Gras rifle, known as "Hotfas". The black powder was made locally, as were the bullets.

In 1937 courses were started in Shihr to upgrade younger irregulars and new recruits from nearby tribes into a cohesive uniformed force called the Gendarmerie. They were still armed with the Le Gras rifle, but some tribesmen had succeeded in acquiring more modern rifles, either .303 Lee Enfields (some marked "Feisal" which had been issued to the Army of the Hejaz in World War I) or 7.92 mm Mausers.

The Qu'aiti Armed Constabulary (Q.A.C.) was formed in about 1949, from the remnants of the Gendamerie. The new force was paid for by the Qu'aiti state and was similar to a rural police force, but armed. The Military Assistant to the Resident Adviser of the Eastern Aden Protectorate, Major Jock Snell, upgraded the new force by arming them with Indian-made .303 Rifles, SMLE No. 1 Mk III. Recruits increasingly came from within the state rather than from Yafa'i. Their commander was Qaid Nasir Awadh al Batati, a local-born Yafa'i. He ran the training depot outside the city of Mukalla, and acted as inspector to the individual provincial forces which served the towns and districts of Shihr, Shibam, Duan, Hajr and the rural areas of Mukalla. Each province possessed a commanding officer. From time to time the officer, N.C.O.'s and men could be transferred between provinces, or to or from headquarters. Jim Ellis, the last Resident Adviser in the Eastern Aden Protectorate, recalls that their effectiveness greatly depended upon how well the provincial governors (*Naibs*) and District Officers (*Qaims*) used them. However, they were generally reliable and far superior to any similar force outside Aden. Many of the force were absorbed successfully into the so-called People's Army following independence.

The Q.A.C. uniform comprised a khaki shirt and shorts and brown leather belt. Headdress consisted of a khaki *imama* with black *aqu'al*. Other ranks had no footwear. No cap badge was worn, but in 1958 a curved brass shoulder title was issued, stamped with the wording "ARMED CONSTABULARY" in Arabic. This was changed to "QU'AITI ARMED CONSTABULARY" in 1962.

Riyan Guards

Haras al Riyan

During the 1940s former slaves and some Somalis were recruited for an airfield protection company known as the "African Company". This was tasked with guarding R.A.F. Riyan, located a few miles outside of Mukalla. To ensure that the company received the necessary military training a King's African Rifles sergeant major was sent to Riyan. The unit, belonging to the Mukalla Regular Army, was commanded by an Indian Army officer. In about 1948 the unit was disbanded, and a new force formed.

The new company undertook the same role, but now consisted of former gendarmerie Yafa'is living in the nearby Boweish village east of Riyan and Seiban tribesmen from the hills to the north. They are reported to have worn sky blue turbans and below-the-knee-length khaki shirts. The commander was a Yafa'i *Mulazim* or lieutenant, who had retired from the Mukalla Regular Army. In about 1960 he was replaced by a Deyyini tribesman from the Hadhrami Bedouin Legion, who had served in the Nizam of Hyderabad's Bodyguard for 17 years before joining the H.B.L. Upon his arrival the Riyan Guards came under H.B.L. influence and changed from M.R.A.-style uniform to that of the H.B.L.

Royal Air Force

The Royal Air Force and Royal Flying Corps became involved with Aden in 1916. It was during that year when the seaplane carrier H.M.S. *Raven II*, which carried six aircraft, was transferred from Port Said, Egypt, to Aden. The ship's aircraft carried out a series of raids on Turkish positions. This demonstration of air power was used both to damage the Turkish war machine and to influence the local Arab population. The latter became a function that was to prove very successful in controlling Aden Protectorate during the 1930s. On 4 April 1928 the Air Ministry assumed responsibility for the defence of Aden from the War Office. This included control of the Aden Protectorate Levies.

In 1928 there were troubles in the Protectorate emanating from Yemen. The previous year Yemen forces were only 40 miles from Aden. Air action was authorised by H.M. Government and the headquarters and garrisons of the military forces of Yemen were bombed. Eventually the Iman evacuated Dhala, which he had previously occupied, and returned to his own country. No.8 Squadron R.A.F. achieved this success in two months. Over the following years the R.A.F. were involved in a number of actions against both incursions of armed tribesmen into Protectorate territory and inter-tribal disturbances. In many cases the threat of air action alone was sufficient to bring about a settlement. Another R.A.F. task was to safeguard Aden against seaborne attack during wartime, and to control and protect the southern approaches to the Red Sea.

At the beginning of the Second World War No.8 Squadron was supplemented with the following squadrons:

11 Squadron (Bombers)
39 Squadron (Bombers)
94 Squadron (Fighters)
203 Ground Reconnaissance Squadron.

A flight of Free French Maryland's also joined the command.

On 12 June 1940 operations commenced against Italian aerodromes in Abyssinia and Eritrea. The Blenheims, Vincents and Gladiators of the command flew reconnaissance, bombing and anti-submarine sweeps. On 19 June 1940 an Italian submarine was attacked by a small naval vessel and a Vincent of No.8 Squadron and surrendered intact. The primary mission of the Aden squadrons was to support the campaigns in Abyssinia. In October 1943 they helped quell rebel elements in Ethiopia. Later in the war a plane from No.8 Squadron assisted in attacking a German U-boat, which was beached and scuttled.

A completely different task arose in 1944 when a famine flight was established to carry food daily to Quatan in the Hadhramaut. This was repeated in early 1949 when famine struck again. Transport aircraft from the Middle East Air Force were sent to R.A.F. Riyan, in Qu'aiti State in the Hadhramaut. From there they carried out an airlift of grain to a secluded valley in the Hadhramaut as thousands of people faced starvation. Between 4 February and 2 March 1949

R.A.F. Dakotas dropped 750 tons of grain, thus averting disaster.

Following the war the R.A.F. in Aden became almost devoid of operational units. Only 621 (G.R.) Squadron, which consisted of Wellingtons, remained at R.A.F. Khormaksar for surveillance of the Red Sea, Gulf of Aden and the Arabian Sea.. During this period the following units were based in South Arabia:

Hedjuff, Aden	Marine Craft Unit, 206, 216 and 220 Air/Sea Rescue Units
Jhadir	Armoured Car Section
Khormaksar	R.A.F. Station comprising:
	621 (G.R.) Squadron (Wellingtons)
	H.Q. B.F. Aden Communication Flight
	1566 Met. Flight
	114 Squadron (Bostons)
Riyan	R.A.F. Station
Shiekh Othman	Aden Protectorate Levies
Socotra	R.A.F. Socotra
Steamer Point	R.A.F. Station comprising:
	Equipment and Supply Section
	50 Embarkation Unit
	7 R.A.F. Hospital
	11 R.A.F. Postal HQ
	3 Base Personnel Office
	6 Works Area
	5721 Mechanical and Electrical Flight
	Aircraft Safety Centre, Southern Arabia
	Area Control, Aden
Wadi Road, Aden	Telecommunications Centre (Aden)

In 1948 the governor requested the deployment of 20 Wing, R.A.F. Regiment to act in an internal security and anti-riot role within the colony. The unit was also tasked with reinforcing Somaliland in the event of an emergency. The wing comprised 58 and 66 field squadrons, with a total strength of about 300 officers and airmen. In addition, a detachment of about 30 was sent to Mweiga, Kenya, as airstrip protection. By 1952 the following units were under the control of H.Q. British Forces in Aden and the Protectorates:

R.A.F. Khormaksar
R.A.F. Steamer Point
R.A.F. Riyan
8 (Light Bomber) Squadron

H.Q. 20 Wing R.A.F. Regiment
H.Q. Aden Protectorate Levies
H.Q. 51st Coast Regiment
H.Q. Troop, 65 Wing, Royal Signals
R.A.F. Hospital Aden
H.Q. British Forces Aden also had functional control of the following units:
114 Maintenance Unit
1152 Marine Craft Unit
50 R.A.F. Movements Unit
Aden Supply Depot

Commitments increased and by the end of 1956 the squadrons in Aden consisted of:

Aden Communications Squadron	8 Valettas and Pembrokes, 2 Sycamores
8 Squadron	16 Venoms
78 Squadron	6 Twin Pioneers
1426 Flight	4 Lincolns
20 Wing R.A.F. Regiment	58 and 66 field squadrons

Over the years the composition of the R.A.F. units in Aden altered as dictated by the circumstances. Operational units permanently located at R.A.F. Khormaksar on 1 January 1964 were as follows:

8 Squadron	12 Hunter GA9
43 Squadron	12 Hunter GA9
208 Squadron	12 Hunter GA9
26 Squadron	7 Belvedere HC1
37 Squadron	4 Shackleton MR2
78 Squadron	8 Twin Pioneer CCI (later Wessex helicopters)
84 Squadron	6 Beverley C1
105 Squadron	10 Argosy C1
233 Squadron	6 Valetta C1
1417 Flight	4 Hunter FR10
SAR Flight	3 Sycamore HR14

While it is not the intention of the authors to provide a detailed analysis of the R.A.F. in Aden, snapshots show the strength of the squadrons and reflect the seriousness of the security situation at a given time. For further information about the role of the Royal Air Force in the Middle East see *Flight From The Middle East*, by Air Marshal Sir David Lee, an excellent and detailed account.

This covers the post-1945 period. Upon the British departure from Aden the squadrons either transferred to other R.A.F. stations in the Gulf or were disbanded.

Royal Navy

Early naval activity in the Aden area was conducted by the Bombay Marine, but the Royal Navy played an increasingly important role during the nineteenth century when the area formed part of the East Indies Station. In 1830 the Bombay Marine became the Indian Navy and following the Indian Mutiny was transferred to the crown in 1858. Five years later it was reduced to non-combatant status. From 1877 onwards it gradually regained its role as a fighting service. For many years there was only a very small naval presence in Aden as it was regarded as little more than an offshoot of the Commander-in-Chief (C-in-C) East Indies Headquarters at Ceylon.

Although Aden possessed a Royal Navy wireless telegraphy station at Khormaksar, it was not until 22 January 1935 that a named naval base, H.M.S. *Norfolk III*, was established. On 1 April 1940 the base was renamed H.M.S. *Sheba*, and located at Tawahi. On 11 June 1941 an expedition was mounted from Aden to capture the Italian-held port of Assab, in Eritrea on the Red Sea, and a contraband control organisation was established. A few enemy submarines were sighted during the war, and early in 1943 a defensive minefield was laid in the Straits of Bab-el-Mandeb. As the war progressed the role of H.M.S. *Sheba* expanded considerably. Its outstations included Port Sudan and Kilindini, the port of Mombassa in Kenya.

From 1945 until 1961, when the unified Middle East Command was instituted, H.M.S. *Sheba*'s importance diminished. This was the first unified, or joint service command introduced post war, and the C-in-C Middle East and his staff was based at Aden. The navy's Arabian Seas and Persian Gulf Station was abolished and the Flag Officer Arabian Seas and Persian Gulf became the Flag Officer Middle East (F.O.M.E.), responsible to the C-in-C Middle East. F.O.M.E. transferred his flag from H.M.S. *Jufair* at Bahrain to H.M.S. *Sheba* in 1962. During the post-war period the Royal Navy was involved in a number of anti-dissident operations in Aden and the Protectorate, principally deploying fixed and rotary wing aircraft of the Fleet Air Arm, and providing support from seaward to land operations. Among these were operations against the tribesmen of the Radfan in 1964, in which 45 Commando Royal Marines participated as an infantry battalion. Helicopters from H.M.S. *Centaur* ferried troops and supplies to the front line, and Sea Vixens flew reconnaissance, photographic and strike sorties against the rebel tribesmen. Royal Naval Fleet

Air Arm and Royal Marine forces continued to be deployed as required during the period of the Emergency. From March 1965 until the withdrawal in 1967 a coastal minesweeper was permanently deployed at Aden in the anti-dissident role.

The withdrawal from Aden in November 1967 marked the end of the Middle East Command and the British civil and military presence in Aden and the protectorate. The High Commissioner and the last British forces finally departed on 29 November. The final phases of the naval withdrawal from Aden were conducted by the Flag Officer Second in Command Far East Fleet at sea, in command of Task Force 318, which provided seaborne cover to the entire operation. TF 318 included an aircraft carrier, commando carrier, 2 assault ships, a guided missile destroyer, 3 frigates, 12 Royal Fleet Auxiliaries, 3 landing ships logistic, 5 landing ships tank, and 42 Commando Royal Marines.

Royal Signals

In 1927 Royal Signals took over the Aden Signal Section from the Indian Signal Corps. Staff at the Royal Signals Museum indicate men were still being posted to the Aden Signal Section as late as 1930, but there is no further mention of this unit in the Corps history of Royal Signals or Indian Signals until 254 Signal Squadron was formed in Aden on 14 September 1959 as the Aden Signal Squadron.

With the increasing need for communications 15 Signal Regiment was re-raised in Aden on 22 January 1965. This regiment absorbed 254 and 255 (Bahrain) Signal Squadrons and 603 Signal Troop. Its role was to provide line and radio communications to the Middle East. It operated against a background of terrorist attacks and civil unrest until disbanded in October 1967. A rearguard squadron remained for a few more weeks. The regiment was located at Singapore Lines, Khormaksar, and provided communications for Aden Brigade and had a troop (F) at Little Aden. A communication centre detachment was located at the F.R.A. camp in Seedaseer Lines and a self-contained radio/cipher detachment was provided for the Resident Adviser in Mukalla. The regiment was able to provide technical personnel, linemen or operators anywhere within South Arabia when required. Its sign was an Egyptian cat with a Roman "15". This reflected the regiment's origin, as it was first raised in Egypt in 1940.

South Arabian Army
Jaish al Janob

On 1 June 1967 the South Arabian Army was formed from the F.R.A. and F.N.G. With the impending departure of Britain from South Arabia it was deemed necessary to consolidate and unify the disparate forces within the country. It was argued that Arabisation was a high priority and rationalisation of the various forces was essential to a successful defence force. It was intended that the Hadhrami Bedouin Legion would also be included when the Eastern Aden Protectorate states joined the Federation. The reality of the merger was that very little change took place, other than the F.R.A. exchanging its head dress for a green beret and a new cap badge and shoulder title. The F.N.G. continued to wear its old badges and beret for some time after amalgamation.

In *Last Post Aden 1964–67* Julian Paget states that on 7 November 1967 the S.A.A. "abandoned their former loyalties to the Federation; they changed their title to the Arab Armed Forces in Occupied South Yemen". British forces rapidly left and by the end of November 1967 all had vacated the country, the former S.A.A. becoming the Army of the People's Democratic Republic of Yemen.

The badge of the S.A.A. was similar to the F.R.A. but with a green scroll and a larger star and crescent. An anodised green shoulder title was issued.

South Arabian Police
Al Shurtah al Arabi'a al Junubiya

Concurrent with the formation of the South Arabian Army on 1 June 1967, the South Arabian Police was formed from the Aden Police and the units of the Federal National Guard 2 (F.N.G.2). Thus it was envisaged that, in one stroke, all of the armed constabularies and police forces of the federation would become a single force. However before this could happen the whole system began to unravel due to the civil war, and many of the old F.N.G.2 units ceased to exist. No dress or insignia changes took place. After the departure of the British from Aden and pending the design and manufacture of a new one, the cap badge was modified by the simple expedient of cutting off the crown.

Tribal Guard
Haras al Qabila

From around 1935 British policy in the protectorates was to encourage state rulers to form their own local armed retinue, or tribal guard, for service within

Tribal Guard at Merta, Western Aden Protectorate, May 1958. He is dressed in a khaki cloth shirt and *footah*, and locally-made sandals. Armed with a S.M.L.E. No.1 Mk III rifle, he carries a locally-produced ammuniton/cartridge belt and has positioned his *jambia* in its traditional place at the front. His head is covered by a plan *Audhali*-style headdress. (Major C. Butt)

their own territory. The rifles and the ammunition were supplied on loan, and remained the property of the Aden Government. By 1940 most of the states had formed their own military units, which were usually officered by friends and relatives of the local ruler. Guards were lightly armed, and in effect constituted a rural constabulary controlled by the local ruler.

The term "tribal guard" usually refers to those forces in the Western Aden Protectorate, but in the Eastern Aden Protectorate the Wahidi Sultanate, and Mahra Sultanate also possessed such forces. Tribal guard existed in the following states: Alawi Sheikhdom, Amirate of Beihan, Upper Aulaqi Sheikhdom, Upper Aulaqi Sultanate, Lower Aulaqi Sultanate, Audhali Sultanate, Dathina Republic, Amirate of Dhala, Shaib Sheikhdom, Muflahi Sheikhdom, Haushabi Sultanate, Lahej Sultanate, Fadhli Sultanate Armed Police and Lower Yafai Sultanate Armed Police. Upper Yafai Sultanate and Aqrabi Sheikhdom did not possess any disciplined forces of any sort. In 1959 the tribal guard merged with the Government Guards, to form the Federal National Guard of the Federation of Arab Amirates of the South.

Tribal guard parade dress comprised a khaki shirt, shorts and red turban. Working dress usually consisted of a khaki cloth shirt, and a *footah* (cotton kilt) with khaki turban. Locally-made kuwash sandals were also worn. Soldiers carried a .303 Rifle, SMLE No.1 Mk III, and wore a locally-made ammunition cartridge belt of leather. The *jambia*, or dagger, was placed in the traditional location at the front of the belt.

On 21 May 1937 the governor of Aden authorised the following uniform for senior and junior tribal guard instructors in the Aden Protectorate:

Khaki shorts; khaki tunic; khaki shirt, and tie; khaki puttees; dark brown boots; plain buttons; red-on-white cloth shoulder badges A.P.T.G. (Aden Protectorate Tribal Guard); red sash; red and green turban flash on khaki turban. Badge: a crescent and star. A leather belt was worn over a dark green cummerbund. The uniform was permitted to be worn on official occasions in the colony of Aden, but it had no relation to the Aden Protectorate Levies, or to any of His Majesty's Forces.

Wahidi Tribal Guard

Haras al Qabila al Wahidi

By about 1886 the British were making treaties with coastal "rulers" along the South Arabian coastline. Some protection would be afforded to the "rulers", in return for them attempting to keep the peace along their various stretches of coast, quelling piracy, and agreeing not sell their land to anyone else. In the area known as Wahidi there were two separate Sultanates – Bir Ali and Balhaf – as well as two apparently independent sheikhdoms of Irqa and Haura Sifla. Treaties were signed with all of them. In 1951 the sheikhdoms were absorbed into the main Wahidi Sultanate of Balhaf and Azzan, but the Bir Ali Sultanate remained separate until the last sultan died in 1967.

During the early twentieth century a degree of anarchy existed. The Balhaf group of sultans managed to hold on to their area, and with the aid of the Jewish population repelled Aulaqi attempts to take over Habban. By 1939, the "Peace of Ingrams" began to be established in Hadhramaut. People were sick and tired of war.

The Wahidi Tribal Guard (W.T.G.) were principally recruited from local tribesmen, but also included several Yafa'is, tribesmen from the Qu'aiti area and one or two Jews from Habban. They were regarded as the "Sultan's men", having played a notable part in the defence of Habban against the Aulaqis. In 1948, a rabbi of Yemeni origin named Zadok visited Habban and urged the Jewish population to return to the "Promised Land". A similar appeal had been made to the Jews of the Yemen. Following negotiations with the sultan and his advisers the great majority decided to go, and travelled to Aden in hired trucks before joining "Operation Magic Carpet" which would take them to Israel. Unlike the Jews of Yemen they were armed with modern rifles and caused quite a stir when they arrived in Aden "zamilling" and firing in the air.

In 1957 Major Jock Snell, the Military Assistant in the area, set about retraining the W.T.G. with Hadhrami Bedouin Legion (H.B.L.) assistance, aiming to make it a more effective force. Gradually the Wahidi administration became settled, and its military force likewise more experienced and dependable. The populated areas became less turbulent and trouble was confined to the mountains of the south-west corner of the state. With H.B.L. garrisons established in the two main inland settlements of Al Khabr and Mit-haf, the area became relatively stable. This enabled the W.T.G. patrols to penetrate the remotest settlements and grazing areas.

Although Wahidi was in the Eastern Aden Protectorate, trade was focused on Aden rather than Mukalla, and when the Federation of South Arabia was founded the Wahidis decided to be come part of the federation. The other Eastern Aden Protectorate states never joined the federation. Consequently the W.T.G. became a part of Federal National Guard II in 1962. As they were a better trained force in a larger area than any of the other federated States, they tended to retain a degree of independence. Their commander, *Qaid* (Major) Mahdi Mohsin Ba Bakri was a Laswadi tribesman from near Habban, and most of the other Wahidi tribes were represented in the force. They protected the security of the state without assistance from Federal National Guard I.

The Wahidi Tribal Guard wore khaki drill shorts and shirts with leather

Airstrip in Wahidi, 1961. This shot was taken following the successful conclusion of a small war with a part of the Qamush tribe, who had thought it their right to raid certain of their neighbours and acquire the goods of travellers without payment. Left to right: Mulazim Hussain bin Afif, W.T.G.; Ahmed al Mardhoof; the Suleimani Muqaddam; Jim Ellis; Ali Sinna, W.T.G. driver; Bin Said; Rubeiya Ba Sa'a; Ike Dawson, Air Liaison Officer; Residency Mechanic; Mehdi Ba Bakri; navigator of the Twin Pioneer; Ahmed bil Hajri; W.T.G. driver; Marzuq (Nkrumah), Bin Said's driver. Bin Said appears to be carrying an 8mm Mauser. (Jim Ellis)

belts. Locally-made leather equipment was worn on patrol. Headdress consisted of green and white *imamas* with black *aqu'al*. After joining the Federal National Guard in 1962 they adopted the dress of that force. The W.T.G. were armed with the .303 Rifle No. 4 Mk I and a few Bren Guns.

Zeylah Field Force

In 1884 an expedition was mounted from Aden to Zeylah (Zeila) on the Somali coast. This field force was raised to relieve the Egyptian garrison of Harrar, fourteen days journey inland from the coast by caravan. The garrison was due to return to Egypt and required support in relinquishing its position, as the situation was unstable. According to the *Illustrated London News* of November 22 1884 the field force sent from Aden consisted of a half-battery of light field artillery (three 7 pdr guns on camels), 150 men of the 4th Bombay Rifles, and a portion of the Aden garrison. The Aden Camel Battery is mentioned by name as a participant.

Appendix I

Comparative Table of Ranks and Rank Illustrations

APL pre-1957	Post-1957	British equivalent rank
	Zaim	Brigadier
	Aqid	Colonel
	Qaid	Lieutenant Colonel
Bimbashi al Alwal	Wakil Qaid	Major
Bimbashi	Rais	Captain
Yuzbashi	Mulazim Awal	Lieutenant
Mulazim	Mulazim Thani	2nd Lieutenant
Sergeant Major	Wakil Dabit Awal	Regimental Sergeant Major
	Wakil Dabit l Imdadat	Regt Quartermaster Sergeant
	Na'qib As Sariya	Company Sergeant Major
Bash Shawoosh	Na'ib Awal	Staff Sergeant
Shawoosh	Na'ib	Sergeant
Wakil	Ar'rif	Corporal
Naib Wakil	Wakil Ar'rif	Lance Corporal
Askar	Jundi	Private

Whilst under R.A.F. command technicians wore inverted chevrons, and this did not change immediately after reverting to army control. The rank Bimbashi al Alwal was not introduced until the late 1950's. The British rank of Major was used prior to this.

Badges of rank of the F.R.A. and the S.A.A.

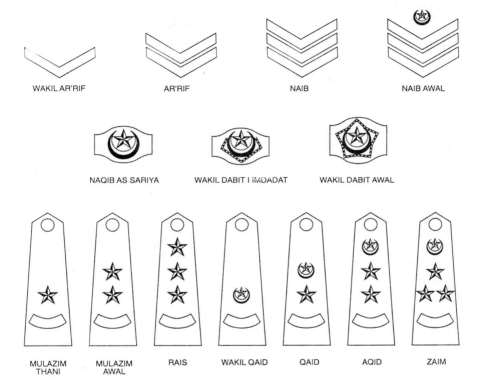

All rank insignia are made of anodised aluminium. The Wakil Qaid, and the Wakil Dabit Awal ranks have green cloth behind the insignia. Green enamel covers the outside edge of the Wakil Dabit Awal rank and the outside edge of the lower half of the Wakil Dabit I Imdadat insignia.

Appendix II

Operations In The Aden Hinterland and The Anglo-Turkish Boundary Commission

When the Turkish Army occupied the Yemen in 1872 it brought them into contact with the British on the Yemen/Aden Protectorate border. This ill-defined boundary became problematic for the British as Yemeni tribes enjoyed raiding into the Protectorate and had to be forcibly removed.

In 1901 tribal disputes arose in the Aden Hinterland near the border. A group of hostile Arabs from Yemen constructed a defensible tower at Ad Dareja in Haushabi territory, which was under British protection. This tower commanded the main trade route and was used as a customs post. Following failed diplomatic correspondence it was destroyed in July by a force sent out from Aden, consisting of 200 men from 1st battalion Royal West Kent Regiment, 200 men from 5th Bombay Light Infantry, half of no.4 company, Bombay Sappers and Miners, and 6 mountain guns from no.16 company, Western Division, Royal Garrison Artillery.

In October 1901 the British and Turkish governments agreed to the demarcation of the frontier between Yemen and the Aden Protectorate. Both Turks and British would appoint a boundary commissioner to be escorted by no more than 200 men. The first meeting took place on 11 February 1902. From the very beginning the Turkish commissioners adopted an uncompromising attitude which bordered upon open hostility. In addition to putting forward preposterous claims, the Turks seized and occupied all territory in dispute. They also increased their garrison at Kataba, 12 miles from Dhala, and strengthened their post at Jalela, which was within 2 miles of the British commission's camp. The two Turkish garrisons totalled about 850 men, equipped with 7 mountain guns and 1 modern field piece.

H.M. Government protests were ineffectual, the Sultan of Dhala appealing to Britain for assistance. In response to the increasing severity of the situation the Aden garrison was reinforced with the 102nd Prince of Wales Grenadiers, a wing of the 123rd Outram's Rifles and the Abbottabad Mountain Battery from India. In addition, the Aden Column was raised, comprising 2nd Royal Dublin Fusiliers, including a section of maxim guns, 12 signallers, a double company of 102nd Grenadiers, and 2 sections of field hospitals. The column left Sheikh Othman on 2 January 1903 with orders to "watch" the frontier. The Aden garrison was not particularly strong and was further reinforced by the Hampshire Regiment, brought in from Lucknow, India. On arrival in Aden five companies were sent to Dhala. A field telegraph was built between Aden and

Dhala, and the roads were improved.

When the British felt secure enough, an ultimatum was presented to the Turkish government, which resulted in all Turkish troops and levies being withdrawn behind the line indicated by the British Commissioner as the approximate frontier of the Aden Protectorate. By March nearly 1,500 British and India soldiers were on the border.

While the border was being surveyed Arab tribes launched numerous raids upon the surveying parties and British troops. A number of punitive actions were taken against Arab villages that supported the warlike tribesmen. The conditions suffered by the troops were very poor. Although casualties from fighting were not high, many suffered from malaria – in the case of the Hampshire's 75% of its strength were afflicted. The Hampshire's regimental history notes that camels provided the transport. Although some of the regiment had experienced camels and their "ways" on the Frontier in India, they discovered the Aden camel – and even more so its driver – to be far more intractable than those they had already encountered.

The following units were to see service with Aden Column, which was raised to provide the Boundary Commission's escort, protect survey parties, and to assist in the protection and building of roads in the Hinterland:

102nd Grenadiers.
94th Russell's Infantry.
123rd Outram's Rifles.
Hampshire Regiment.
Buffs, East Kent Regiment.
2nd Royal Dublin Fusiliers.
30th Mountain Bty. (later 10th Abbotabad Mountain Bty.).
Camel Bty. (two 5 pdr. guns drawn by camels and manned by the
    R.G.A. from Aden).
6 (British) Mountain Bty.
45 Coy R.G.A.
Aden Troop.
Section A., no. 16 British Field Hospital.
Section A., no. 68 Native Field Hospital.

When the Boundary Commission entered Subaihi territory a flying column was organised from the troops at Musemir, and a second force known as the Subaihi Column was mobilised at Aden to join them. On 1 March 1904 the Aden Column was broken up, although troops were temporarily retained at Dhala and along the line of communications. As the Boundary Commission approached the coast it used Ras Ara, 70 miles west of Aden, as its base, and 350 men from 94th Russell's Infantry were located there until the delimitation work was completed in May.

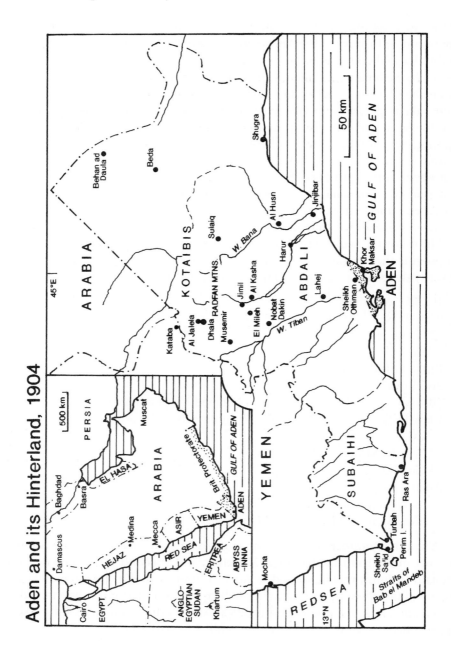

Aden and its Hinterland, 1904

Appendix III

British Military Forces In Aden 1914–1919

Upon their entry into the First World War in 1914, reports were received that the Turks were building up their forces in the Sheikh Said peninsula, opposite Perim Island, and contemplating action against the Aden Protectorate.

On 3 November 1914 29th Indian Infantry Brigade, en-route to Suez, received orders to capture Sheikh Said. Seven days later the brigade, assisted by 23rd Pioneers landed and drove the enemy inland. Turkish field guns were captured, and Turbah Fort and other enemy works were demolished. No further action occurred in this area until 14 June 1915 when 23rd Pioneers successfully resisted an attempted landing on Perim Island.

On 4 July 1915 the Aden Movable Column, including Aden Troop, moved to Lahej, which was being threatened by the Turks. An engagement took place that evening, but due to transport difficulties and severe heat the column was forced to withdraw as far as Khormaksar, Sheikh Othman falling to the Turks. As a consequence the Aden garrison was strengthened with the arrival of the 28th Indian Brigade from Egypt, which consisted of 51st Sikhs, 53rd Sikhs, 56th Punjabis, 62nd Punjabis and 2 batteries of horse artillery. On 21 July the brigade, supported by troops from the Aden garrison including a detachment of Sappers and Miners and the Aden Troop, surprised and routed the Turks at Sheikh Othman. Several hundred Turkish soldiers were captured. The brigade enjoyed further success on the August 24, when the enemy garrison at Fiyush was forced to retire on Lahej; four days later a similar success was gained at Waht. During the remainder of the year further skirmishes occurred, the infantry averting a threatened advance upon Imad.

During 1916 the Movable Column inflicted considerable loss on a Turkish force near Subar, thus securing the tribes to the east. On 16 March 1916 the Turks attacked Imad in force, but were beaten off without difficulty. Later that year, on 7 December, the Turkish posts at Jabir and Mahat were attacked, the enemy suffering about 200 casualties.

On 1 June 1917 the seaplane carrier H.M.S. *Raven II* arrived, its aircraft undertaking a bombing and reconnaissance flight that same afternoon. The aircraft were of immense value despite only being on station for a short time. Further skirmishing was to take place until the end of the war. Although it could be argued that the Turks blockaded Aden throughout the war, it was British policy to employ a smaller force of British troops in keeping the larger Turkish forces tied up in Lahej for the duration, thus preventing them causing trouble in Yemen.

The following list contains the principal British, Indian, Malay and Arab units serving in Aden from 1914 to 1919. The British infantry battalion was usually replaced each year while the Indian battalions often stayed much longer. Royal Garrison Artillery companies also rotated on a regular basis.

Indian Army Order No. 618-1916 stated that the title of the G.O.C. Aden (Independent) Bde. would change to G.O.C. Aden. It also stated the infantry brigade and its various attached units, forming the Movable Column, would be known as "the Aden Infantry Brigade". The troops under the command of the G.O.C. Aden would be known as the Aden Field Force.

Royal Flying Corps

½ flight No. 114 Sqn R.F.C.
No. 57 Kite Balloon Section R.F.C.

Cavalry

26th Indian Cavalry.
Aden Troop (Punjabis).

Artillery

61 Coy R.G.A. (Coastal Artillery).
62 Coy R.G.A.
69 Coy R.G.A.
70 Coy R.G.A (Coastal Artillery).
76 Coy R.G.A (Coastal Artillery).
85 Coy R.G.A.
10-pdr Camel Battery R.G.A.
15-pdr Camel Bty R.G.A.
5" battery R.G.A.
2/1/Devon (H) Bty.
4/Hants (H) Bty.
1105(H) Bty.
Malay States Guides Mountain Bty.
Aden Ammunition Column.

Engineers

5 Coy Bengal Sappers and Miners.
6 Engineer Field Park Bengal S&M.
23 (Fortress) Coy, 3 Bombay S&M.
51 Coy 1st Bengal S&M.
Aden Defence Light Section, Bombay S&M.

Signals

Aden Signal Coy, Bombay S&M.
½ troop, Pack Wireless.

Infantry

1/Royal Irish Rifles.
1/Lancs.
1/Brecknock South Wales Borderers.
4/Buffs.
4/D.C.L.I.
6/East Surreys.
7/Hampshires.
1st Brahmans.
7th Rajput.
23rd Sikh Pioneers (from 29 Bde.).
33rd Punjabis.
38th Dogras.
45 (Aden) Rifles.
62nd Punjabis (from 28 Bde).
69th Punjabis.
75th Carnatics.
2/101st Grenadiers.
108th Infantry.
109th Infantry.
126th Baluchis (from 30 Bde).
Malay States Guides.
1st Yemen Infantry.
Aden Machine Gun Company.

Medical Services

2 Section British General Hospital.
No.10 British Stationary Hospital.
No.10 Advanced Depot of Medical Stores.
No.10 British Staging Section Casualty Clearing Station.
Section B No.24 British Field Ambulance.
Section B No.26 British Field Ambulance.
Section A No.26 Indian General Hospital.
Section B No.26 Indian General Hospital.
No.80 Indian Stationary Hospital.

No.80 Indian Staging Section Casualty Clearing Station.
2 sections 105 Indian Field Ambulance plus 1 British section.
Section C No.133 Indian Field Ambulance.
Section D No.133 Indian Field Ambulance.
Section A No.138 Indian Field Ambulance.
Section B No.138 Indian Field Ambulance.
Section A No.138 Combined Field Ambulance.
Section B No.138 Combined Field Ambulance.
No.138 Combined Field Ambulance.
Benares Ambulance Transport Section.

Veterinary Services

Field Veterinary Section.

Supply and Transport

Supply and Transport Office.
Detachment 7 Mule Corps.
18 Pack Corps (became 18 Pack Mule Corps in 1921).
56 Camel Company (Siladar).
Aden Mechanical Transport Section.
Aden Labour Corps.
Porter Corps.
Aden Water Column.
No.31 Divisional Supply Company.
No.53 Bde. Supply Section.
No.55 Supply and Transport H.Q. (Line of Communication).
No.108 Bde. Supply Section.
"T" Supply Depot Company.

Ordnance

Ordnance Field Park.
Ordnance Advance Depot.
Detachment Indian Ordnance Depot.

Temporary Troops

28 (Frontier Force) Indian Brigade, comprising:
    51st Sikhs.
    53rd Sikhs.
    56th Punjabis.
    62nd Punjabis.

Berkshire Battery R.H.A. (T).
"B" Battery Honourable Artillery Company.
29 Indian Brigade, comprising:
57th Rifles.
Patiala Infantry.
23rd Sikh Pioneers.
30 Indian Brigade:
½ 126th Baluchis.
Australian Light Horse (disembarked from troop ship for short period).
9th Gurkha Rifles (double company disembarked from troop ship for
short period).
Machine Gun Detachment, and Wireless Section, HMS *Philomel*.

Appendix IV

Turkish Yemen Army Corps, 1916

In February 1916 the principal units of the Turkish Army in Yemen were:

39th Division, Taiz

115th Infantry Regiment.
116th Infantry Regiment (part).
117th Infantry Regiment.
119th Infantry Regiment (part).
7th Model Battalion.

40th Division, Hodeida

118th Infantry Regiment.
119th Infantry Regiment (part).
120th Infantry Regiment.

Corps Troops

26th Cavalry Regiment.
Horse artillery battalion.
3 machine gun companies.
9 field and mountain batteries.
Howitzer battery.
4 heavy batteries.
7th Engineer Battalion.
Independent engineer company.
Rocket battery.

There also were a large number of Arab auxiliaries and two militia battalions.

The following Turkish units were in the Protectorate in 1916:

Lahej

1st Battalion, 117th Infantry Regiment.
Elements of 26th Cavalry Regiment.
A number of guns.

Waht

2nd Battalion, 115th Infantry Regiment.
3rd Battalion, 115th Infantry Regiment.

3rd Battalion, 116th Infantry Regiment.
2nd Battalion, 117th Infantry Regiment.
3rd Battalion, 117th Infantry Regiment.
Machine gun company (5 machine guns).
Independent engineer company.
Battery of 4 x 7.7cm guns and 1 mortar attached.
Battery of 2 x howitzers.
2 mountain batteries, one probably Q.F.

Subar

3rd Battalion, 119th Infantry Regiment.
7th Model Battalion.
2 x machine guns.
Mountain battery.

Sheikh Said

1st Battalion, 120th Regiment.
Mountain battery.
Half 10.5cm battery of two guns.

Appendix V

British Military Forces In Aden 1939–45

H.Q. British Troops Aden, 3 September 1939

H.Q. Royal Artillery Aden.
Detachment, 8th Anti-Aircraft Battery, Royal Artillery.
9th Heavy Battery, R.A.
20th Fortress Company, R.E.
2/5th Mahratta Light Infantry – Khormaksar.
Aden Protectorate Levies – Khormaksar.
Independent Flight Armoured Cars, R.A.F.

British Military Forces in Aden 1939–45, excluding locally-raised forces

2/5th Mahratta Light Infantry – left Aden in August 1940 and arrived at Port Sudan on 23 August.
1/2nd Punjab Regiment – Arrived in Aden in May 1940. Moved to British Somaliland on 29 June 1940, returning to Aden on 18 August.

3/15th Punjab Regiment – Arrived in Aden in July 1940. Served in British Somaliland from July until 16 August 1940, when it returned to Aden.

2nd Battalion, The Black Watch – Arrived at Khormaksar on 1 July 1940. Served in British Somaliland from 6 to 19 August 1940 and returned to Aden. Left Aden for Suez on 26 August.

1st Battalion, Northern Rhodesia Regiment – Withdrawn from British Somaliland on 16 August 1940, remaining in Aden until 17 September.

3/7th Rajput Regiment – arrived in Aden during August 1940, left the following month. Returned in December 1942, remaining until May 1944.

2/10th Gurkha Rifles – May–December 1942.

3/1st Punjab Regiment – Arrived in November 1942, relocated to Socotra in April 1943.

Mewar Bhopal Infantry (Indian State Forces) – December 1942–May 1944.

1st Rampur Infantry (I.S.F.) – May–November 1944.

1st Hyderabad Lancers (I.S.F.) – November 1944–December 1945.

1st Patiala Lancers (I.S.F.) – December 1945–1946.

Somaliland Camel Corps – Withdrawn from British Somaliland on 16 August 1940 and sent to Aden. Left Aden by 17 September 1940.

Bikanir Ganga Risala I.S.F. Camel unit – Sent to Aden from India on 8 September 1940, returning in 1942.

H.Q.R.A. Aden – 1 March 1944–31 December 1944.

5th Heavy Regiment, R.A. – formed 8 September 1939 in Aden.

9th (Minden) Heavy Battery, R.A.

15th AA Battery, Hong Kong Singapore Royal Artillery – formed 8 September 1939.

23rd AA Battery, H.K.S.R.A. – arrived 23 February 1940 from Singapore. This battery served in British Somaliland from 6–16 August 1940.

24th Searchlight Battery, H.K.S.R.A. – formed 30 March 1940.

9th Coast Battery – 14 December 1940 – 17 May 1945.

9th Coast Battery South Arabian – 17 May – 31 December 1945.

5th Coast Regiment – 14 December 1940 – 1 March 1944. Reformed as 1st Heavy Anti-Aircraft Artillery Regiment, H.K.S.R.A. The A.A. batteries became H.A.A. batteries on 1 June 1940.

18th Mountain Battery, Indian Army – left India for Aden on 23 October 1940.

27th Mountain Battery, Indian Army – raised in India 1 December 1939, and moved to Aden. Left Aden for East Africa during August 1940.

20th Fortress Company, R.E.

Detachment Royal Indian Army Service Corps.

17th Indian Staging Section.

This information was kindly prepared by David A. Ryan.

Appendix VI

British Military Forces In Aden 1964–67

In 1963 an insurgent organisation entitled the National Liberation Front (N.L.F.) was created. Enjoying backing from Egypt, the organisation's head-quarters were in Taiz, Yemen. On 14 October 1963 a decision was made to shift from a policy based on politics to one of violent "revolutionary struggle". This became clear when a bomb attack occurred against the High Commissioner and Federal ministers at Khormaksar Airport on 10 December 1963. A state of emergency was declared which lasted until the British left at the end of 1967. By this time Aden had become a very important military base. In 1960 Headquar-ters Middle East Command had located itself there and four years later 24 Infantry Brigade was to move to Little Aden after relocating from Kenya.

The N.L.F.'s insurgents infiltrated across the border into South Arabia where they were tasked with creating mayhem throughout the country. Their path was prepared by a propaganda war run by Egypt using Cairo Radio, and two radio stations in Yemen, Radio Sana and Radio Taiz. Clever and enter-taining programmes were transmitted to the people of South Arabia, which gradually indoctrinated them into the politics of Egypt and Arab nationalism. The nationalists also encouraged tribesmen to take up arms against govern-ment forces by bribing them with new rifles. This subversion was increasingly successful, government forces suffering many attacks on border forts whilst convoys on the Dhala Road frequently encountered both landmines and ambushes.

British and Federal forces quickly drew up a plan to combat these problems. This became known as the Radfan Campaign, being named after the Radfan mountains where the dissidents were gathered. An ad hoc brigade-strength formation, known as RADFORCE, was cobbled together. Its brief was to place troops in the Radfan area and evict the warring tribesmen, denying them access to fertile areas, and their routes to the Yemen. Consisting essentially of moun-tain warfare, operations began on 30 April 1964. On 11 May 1964, 39 Brigade took over from RADFORCE, when the former's headquarters was flown in from Northern Ireland. By 11 June the campaign was over. During October the brigade was replaced by 24 Brigade. Although the Radfan campaign was a mili-tary success for the British, worldwide press coverage provided much hostile propaganda against Britain and the Federation. Although trouble continued to flare up, both on the border and in the mountains, it was on a lesser scale after the Radfan Campaign.

Nationalist organisations also chose to support a campaign of terrorism in

Aden. The 1964 British declaration which stated that they would leave Aden "not later than 1968" caused the various nationalist bodies to vie for power, each hoping they would be the rulers of the country following Britain's withdrawal. The major terrorist organisations were F.L.O.S.Y. and the N.L.F. Although F.L.O.S.Y. was very strong in Aden State, the N.L.F. eventually took control. Without a doubt, the terrorist propaganda and intimidation was very successful. Nevertheless, British and Federal forces succeeded in curbing terrorism and enabled the British Government to negotiate from a position of some strength. Aden Brigade was responsible for internal security in Aden State, whilst 24 Infantry Brigade, stationed in Little Aden, was given the task of providing forces for "up country" within the Federation, although they could be called on to assist in Aden. The military forces in Aden State performed a policeman's role under very different circumstances to their colleagues "up country". They had to cope with urban terrorism as opposed to the campaign in the Radfan, which resembled soldiering on the old North West Frontier of India. Considerable restraint and discipline was shown by all, without which a successful withdrawal in November 1967 would not have been possible.

Commands and Formations

Middle East Command – H.Q. moved to Aden 1 March 1961. Disbanded 29 November 1967.

Aden Brigade – served as Aden garrison.

39 Brigade – H.Q. arrived from Northern Ireland on 11 May 1964 and took command of units already in Aden. Returned to UK during October 1964.

24 Brigade – H.Q. arrived from East Africa during October 1964, while its units went home. Took over units of 39 Brigade.

Artillery

1st Light Regt. R.H.A. (18 September 1965–20 April 1966).

1st Regt. R.H.A. (20 April 1966–20 June 1967).

19th Light Regt. (August 1964–August 1965).

J Battery, 3rd R.H.A. (18 March–1 May 1964).

170 (Imjin) Bty., 7th Regt. R.H.A. (1964, one troop).

20 Commando (Amphibious Observation) Bty. (5 May–31 December 1964).

67 Field Bty. (8 May–29 June 1964).

28 Medium Bty. (9 May–19 June 1964).

25 Field Bty. (9 May–19 June 1964).

25 Light Bty. (19 June 1964–1 September 1965).

67 Light Bty. (29 June 1964–1 September 1965).

28 Light Bty. (1 January–10 September 1965).

G Para Bty. R.H.A. (1 April–1 May 1965).
F Para Bty. R.H.A. (1 May–15 October 1965).
E Bty. R.H.A. (1 September 1965–1 June 1967).
B Bty. R.H.A. (1 September 1965–1 June 1967).
A Bty. R.H.A. (1 September 1965–1 June 1967).
4 Light Bty. (1 April–1 July 1967).
3 Light Bty. (1 May–1 September 1967).
31 Light Bty. (1 June–1 November 1967).
8 Cdo Light Bty. (1 October–1 November 1967).
7 Cdo Light Bty. (1 November 1967–1 February 1968).
47 Light Regt. (June–August 1967).

Engineers

2 Field Survey Depot (1963-1966).
3 Field Sqdn. R.E. (1963-1967).
6 Field Park Sqdn. (1964-1965).
9 (Para) Field Sqdn. R.E. (1964-1965).
10 Airfield Sqdn. R.E. (1965-1967).
12 Field Sqdn. R.E. (1963-1964).
13 Field Survey Sqdn. (1963-1966).
15 Field Park Sqdn. (1963-1964).
19 Topographical Sqdn. (1963-1966).
20 Field Sqdn. (1965-1966).
24 Field Sqdn. R.E. (1964-1965).
30 Field Sqdn. R.E. (1966-1967).
32 Field Sqdn. (1963).
34 Field Sqdn. R.E. (1 troop).
39 Field Sqdn. R.E. (1967).
48 Field Sqdn. R.E. (1963-1964).
50 Field Sqdn. R.E. (troop 1964-1965).
60 Field Sqdn. R.E. (1964-1965).
63 Field Pk Sqdn. R.E. (1964-1967).
73 Field Sqdn. R.E. (1965).
261 Postal Unit.
300 Field Sqdn., 131 Para Engineer Regt T.A. (1965).
513 Specialist Team Royal Engineers.
516 Petrol Oil Lubricants (P.O.L) (1964-1965).
521 S.T.R.E. Well Drilling (1964-1965).
523 S.T.R.E. Works Agency.

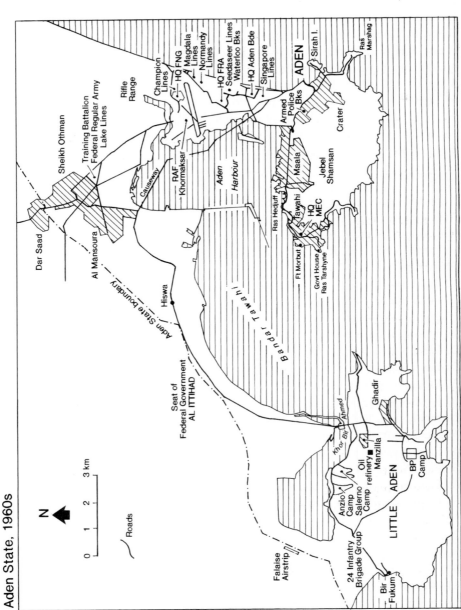

Aden State, 1960s

Signals

15th Signal Regiment (1965-1967).
39 Infantry Brigade Signal Sqdn. (1964).
24 Infantry Brigade Signal Sqdn. (1964-1967).
254 Signal Sqdn. (1959-1965).

Armour

16th/5th Queen's Royal Lancers (one troop).
5th Royal Inniskilling Dragoon Guards (December 1964–December 1965).
D Sqdn., 4th Royal Tank Regiment (April 1964–August 1964).
10th Royal Hussars (August 1964–August 1965).
4th/7th Royal Dragoon Guards (August 1965–September 1966).
1st Royal Tank Regiment (December 1965–1967).
1st Queen's Dragoon Guards (September 1966–July 1967).
Queen's Own Hussars (July 1967–October 1967).

Infantry

1st East Anglian Regiment (February 1964–September 1965).
1st King's Own Scottish Borderers (April 1964–July 1964).
2nd Coldstream Guards (October 1964–October 1965).
1st Royal Scots (October 1964–August 1965).
1st Royal Sussex Regiment (April 1965–October 1965).
4th Royal Anglian Regiment (February 1965–August 1965).
1st King's Own Yorkshire Light Infantry (August 1965–May 1966).
1st Prince of Wales's Own Regiment of Yorkshire (September 1965–Sepember 1966, June 1967–November 1967).
1st Welsh Guards (October 1965–October 1966).
1st Coldstream Guards (October 1965–April 1966).
1st Somerset and Cornwall Light Infantry (April 1966–October 1966).
3rd Royal Anglian Regiment (October 1966–May 1967).
1st Cameronians (May 1966–February 1967).
1st Royal Northumberland Fusiliers (September 1966–June 1967).
1st Irish Guards (October 1966–August 1967).
1st Lancashire Regiment (February 1967–August 1967).
1st Parachute Regiment (May 1967–November 1967).
3rd Parachute Regiment.
1st South Wales Borderers (January 1967–November 1967).
1st Argyll and Sutherland Highlanders (June 1967–November 1967).

Royal Marines

45 Commando, R.M. (April 1964–August 1967).
42 Commando, R.M. (11th October–November 1967).

Single detached companies

A Sqdn., 22nd Special Air Service (April 1964–1966).
1st Gloucestershire Regiment.
1st Royal Irish Fusiliers (1966).
1st Loyals.
C Coy, 1st King's Own Royal Border Regiment (February 1967–November 1967).
Royal Corps of Transport.
51 Port Squadron.
60 Sqdn.
Royal Pioneer Corps.
518 Coy.
Army Air Corps.
13 Flight, 653 Squadron.
Joint Services Port Unit.

The authors are indebted to Todd Mills and Frank Stevens for the order-of-battle information.

Appendix VII

Badges and Insignia of the Armed Forces of Aden

1st YEMEN INFANTRY/ADEN POLICE   Left to right: Brass shoulder title, 1st Yemen Infantry (Tom Wylie); Silver brooch, 1st Yemen Infantry (Tom Wylie); Aden Police headdddress badge, with a white metal Tudor crown, worn until 1954 (Cliff Lord); Aden Police headdress badge, officer's issue, with blue enamel and St Edward's crown, worn 1954–67 (Cliff Lord).

ADEN POLICE   Left to right: Aden Police headdress badge bearing white metal St Edward's crown, worn 1954–67; Aden Police belt buckle. This heavy base metal buckle was worn on a black leather belt. The Tudor crown is surmounted by the curved inscription ADEN POLICE. After 1954, the Tudor crown was replaced by the St Edward's crown. The officer's number is stamped below the crown; Aden Police monogram as worn on fez (all photos Cliff Lord).

ADEN POLICE   Left to right: First type of Aden Police collar badge; Second type of Aden Police collar badge, voided and non-voided styles; Aden Police title large; Aden Police title small (all photos Cliff Lord).

ADEN POLICE/A.P.L.   Left to right: Aden Police button, post-1953; Aden Police officer's rank insignia, post-1953; A.P.L. headdress badge; A.P.L. collar badge; A.P.L. shoulder title (all photos Cliff Lord).

A.P.L./F.N.G.   Left to right: Unofficial A.P.L. cloth shoulder title, green with white lettering (R.H. Daly); Unofficial A.P.L. headdress badge, worn by R.A.F. personnel during the 1950s (David Birtles); F.N.G. cap badge, of brass or white metal (Cliff Lord).

F.N.G. Left to right: F.N.G. shoulder title, brass or white metal (Cliff Lord); F.N.G. officers' issue cloth shoulder title. Brown script on green felt (Cliff Lord); F.N.G. officers' white metal cap and collar badges (Tom Wylie).

F.N.G. Tribal insignia for (left to right): Al Muflahi Sheikhdom; Al Fadli Sultanate; Lower Aulaqi Sultanate. Khaki drill with black script, sealed 10 February 1961 (all photos Tom Wylie).

F.N.G. Tribal insignia for (left to right): Al Audali Sultanate; Upper Aulaqi Sheikhdom; Dathina. Khaki drill with black script, sealed 10 February 1961 (all photos Tom Wylie).

F.N.G. Tribal insignia for (left to right): Ad Dala Emirate; Lower Yafa Sultanate; Beiham Emirate. Khaki drill with black script, sealed 10 February 1961 (all photos Tom Wylie).

F.N.G./F.R.A. Left to right: Tribal insignia for Al Abdali Sultanate (Abdali being the family name of the Lahej sultans). Khaki drill with black script, sealed 10 February 1961 (Tom Wylie); F.R.A. headdress badge (Cliff Lord); F.R.A. collar badge (Cliff Lord); F.R.A. shoulder title (Cliff Lord).

F.R.A./GOVERNMENT GUARDS Left to right: F.R.A. anodised aluminium shoulder title in gold (Cliff Lord); G.G. headdress badge of cast brass or bronze. The badge bears a St Edward's Crown (Cliff Lord); G.G. officers' issue head-dress badge of die-cast bronze, manufactured by Firmin of London (Tom Wylie); G.G. blackened brass shoulder title. Crown Agents pattern no. 442, sealed 21 May 1947 (Tom Wylie).

GOVERNMENT GUARDS   Left to right: G.G. cloth shoulder titles. Arabic titles read "Government Guard". Black script on green felt for officers, black-on-khaki for other ranks; G.G. marksman's badge. Black rifles on khaki drill backing. (photos Tom Wylie).

H.B.L./KATHIRI A.C./MUKALLA PRISON   Left to right: H.B.L. white metal headdress badge (Tom Wylie); Variant of the H.B.L. headdress badge, of cast white metal. Of local manufacture, this had a brooch pin fastening (MHS Bulletin #166); K.A.C. brass shoulder title bearing a black inscription (Tom Wylie); Mukalla Prison Police brass shoulder title produced by Firmin of London. Crown Agents Pattern 708, 1964 (Tom Wylie).

M.R.A./QU'AITI A.C   Left to right: M.R.A. brass shoulder title. Die-cast by Firmin, London, 1947. Crown Agents Pattern 527; M.R.A. Qu'aiti Military Band. Produced by Dowler of Birmingham, 1960. Crown Agents Pattern 6998 7/4/60; Brass title as worn by Q.A.C. until 1962. Crown Agents Pattern 6190 17/3/58; Qu'aiti A.C. brass title, 1962. Crown Agents Pattern 9901 (all photos Tom Wylie).

S.A. ARMY/QU'AITI D.S.M Left to right: S.A.A. beret badge. This anodised aluminium badge is silver with gold star and *jambia* hilts. The scroll is of green enamel; S.A.A. anodised shoulder title, silver inscription on green enamel; Qu'aiti D.S.M. and Meritorious Service Medal, obverse; Qu'aiti D.S.M. and Meritorious Service Medal, reverse (all photos Cliff Lord).

Appendix VIII

Order of the Morning Star, Lahej

Wissam Najmat al-Sabah

Apparently awarded only once, the Order of the Morning Star represents an interesting tale. In 1910 the Egyptian photographer Riad Shihata visited Lahej to take photographs of the ruler. When the work was completed, Shihata was consulted regarding his reward and told Sultan Ahmad that he would accept a decoration. Thus, the Order of the Morning Star was created to meet the photographer's request. Riad Shihata was allowed to design the award and to undertake the manufacture of the badge.

Obverse:	A seven-pointed silver rayed star suspended by a crown, with a central silver medallion, red with a silver dagger point to the left. Around the centre an Arabic inscription "AHMAD BIN FADHL AL-ABDALAI SULTAN LAHEJ/1329".
Reverse:	Plain.
Ribbon:	Unknown.
Awards:	As far as is known, the only award was to its initiator, Riad Shihata.
Established:	1329 (A.H. = 1910 C.E.) by Sultan Ahmad bin Fadhl Mohsin al-Abdali.

The authors are indebted to Owain Raw-Rees for this information.

Appendix IX

Qu'aiti Distinguished Service Medal and Meritorious Service Medal

These medals were awarded sparingly by Sultan Saleh and his successors Sultan Awadh and Sultan Ghalib until November 1967 when the British Government unilaterally handed over authority to the National Liberation Front, and Sultan Ghalib was forced into exile. In 1966 a commission had been set up by Sultan Ghalib to review the Qu'aiti honours system but with his exile in 1967 this was never occurred.

Obverse: An effigy of Saleh bin Ghalib Al Qu'aiti, the Sultan of Shiher and Mukalla, the ruler of the Qu'aiti State in the Hadhramaut, in ceremonial dress.

Reverse: The Arms of the Sultan being the cipher of the Sultan supported by a lion, to the left, and a unicorn. Above this are two crossed sabres, hilts downward. Below the cipher, on a scroll, is the inscription, in English only – "H.H. SULTAN SIR SALEH BIN GHALIB AL QU'AITI, SULTAN OF SHIHER AND MUKALLA, KCMG". At the top of the D.S.M. is the Arabic inscription: "ORDER OF EXCELLENCE". At the top of the M.S.M. is the Arabic inscription: "ORDER OF MERIT".

Size: 36mm in diameter.

Metal: D.S.M. Silver; M.S.M. Bronze.

Ribbon: 31.5mm wide. The civil version has three equal stripes of red, yellow and blue whilst the military ribbons have a central 2mm wide white stripe. These colours echo the national flag – the red being the old Yafa'i colour, the yellow for the desert, and the blue for the sea.

Suspension: D.S.M. – a scroll bar fixed clamp; M.S.M. – a plain bar fixed clamp.

Designer: Mr Percy Metcalfe modelled the obverse, the initials P.M. being visible at the base of the obverse. The reverse was prepared by the Royal Mint based on an image supplied by the Sultanate.

Manufacturer: The Royal Mint, London.

Instituted: 2 October 1948.

The authors are indebted to Owain Raw-Rees for this information

Appendix X

General Service Medal 1918–1962, with Clasp "Arabian Peninsula"

The G.S.M. with clasp "Arabian Peninsula" was awarded for service in resisting border raids, and operations against bands of dissidents in the Arabian Peninsula between 1 January 1957 and 30 June 1960 inclusive. Service of 30 days was required. The medal was authorised by A.O. No.4 19 January 1923. Six issues of the medal exist. The sixth issue 1953-1964 is described thus:

Obverse: Crowned bust of Queen Elizabeth II and the inscription "ELIZABETH II DEI GRATIA REGINA F.D."

Reverse: Winged figure of Victory, standing and placing a wreath on the emblems of the two services. In her left hand is a trident.

Metal: Silver 36mm diameter.

Ribbon: 32mm wide purple with a green strip in the centre.

Suspension: Ornamental swivelling suspender.

Designer: E. Carter Preston.

Clasp: Arabian Peninsula authorised by A.O. 9, 22 February 1961. A total of 16 clasps for different campaigns were issued.

The following local units were entitled to the G.S.M. 1918–62 and the clasp Arabian Peninsula:

Aden Protectorate Government

Aden Protectorate Levies.
Government Guards.
Hadhrami Bedouin Legion.

Eastern Protectorate

Mukalla Regular Army.
Qu'aiti Armed Constabulary.
Kathiri Armed Constabulary.
Wahidi Tribal Guards.

Western Protectorate

For the period 1 January 1957–11 February 1959:
    Amiri Tribal Guards.
    Beihan Tribal Guards.
    Upper Aulaqi Sheikdom Tribal Guards.
    Aughali Tribal Guards.
    Fadhli Armed Police.
    Lower Yafai Armed Police.

For the period 1 January 1957 – 11 February 1960:
    Lower Aulaqi Sultanate Tribal Guards.
    Dathina Tribal Guards.

For the period 1 January 1957 – 30 June 1960:
    Upper Aulaqi Sultanate Tribal Guards.
    Shu'aibi Tribal Guards.
    Muflahi Tribal Guards.
    Haushabi Tribal Guards.

For the period 1 April 1959 – 5 October 1959:
    Lahej Regular Army.
    Lahej Tribal Guards.

For the period 11 February 1959 – 30 June 1960:
    (Federation of Arab Amirates of the South).
    Federal National Guard.

Authors' note: The spelling of some state names in this list differs from the map.

Appendix XI

Campaign Service Medal 1962–Present

This medal superseded both the Naval General Service Medal 1915 and the 1918 Army and R.A.F. General Service Medal, and was instituted by Ministry of Defence Order No. 61, 6 October 1964.

Obverse:	Crowned bust of Queen Elizabeth II and an inscription "ELIZABETH II DEI GRATIA REGINA F.D."
Reverse:	Wreath of oak surrounding the words "FOR CAMPAIGN SERVICE".
Metal:	Cupro-nickel 36mm diameter.
Ribbon:	32mm wide. Purple with green edges.
Suspension:	Ornamental swivelling suspender.
Designer:	T.H. Paget, O.B.E.

South Arabian clasps to the medal were:

RADFAN

This was issued to all British and Federal forces participating in 14 days continuous service in South Arabia either during the Radfan operation itself, or whilst operating in a supporting role. The qualifying period was 25 April to 31 July 1964. Authorised by A.O. 36/65.

SOUTH ARABIA

This was awarded for 30 days continuous service in South Arabia, between 1 August 1964 and 30 November 1967. Authorised by A.O. 40/66.

Appendix XII

Orders, Decorations and Medals of the Federation of South Arabia

It would appear that these orders, decorations and medals were instituted by the Supreme Council in 1963 or early 1964. In all instances the awards were designed by the Permanent Secretary to the Ministry of Defence of the Federation, Colonel J.B. Chaplain D.S.O., O.B.E. The manufacture was undertaken by Spink and Son of St. James's, London.

The following awards, listed in order of precedence, were announced on 16 March 1964:

Gallantry Medal 1st Class.
The Order of South Arabia 1st Class.
The Order of South Arabia 2nd Class.
The Order of South Arabia 3rd Class.
The Order of South Arabia 4th Class.
Gallantry Medal 2nd Class.
The Order of South Arabia Medal.
Military Service Medal.
Long Service and Good Conduct Medal.

Also awarded by the Supreme Council were:
(a) Supreme Council Commendation.
To mark acts of bravery performed by any persons which do not entail a gallantry award but nevertheless involve risk to life and merit recognition.
(b) Certificate of Meritorious Service.

The Order of South Arabia

Obverse: (a) Badge. A seven-pointed star with a circular centre depicting an upturned crescent entwined with cloth, between the tips of the crescent a five-pointed star, below which is a sheathed dagger.
(b) Breast Star. A seven-pointed rayed star with a central medallion bearing a similar design to the badge surmounted by the inscription "HERO OF THE ORDER OF SOUTH ARABIA". Surrounding the central medallion are 7 spaced five-pointed stars.

Reverse: (a) Badge. Plain.
(b) Breast Star. Plain.

Classes: Five, both civil and military.

Size: 1st Class Star 85 mm diameter.
2nd Class – no details available.
3rd Class Badge 44 mm diameter.
4th Class Badge 44mm diameter.
5th Class Badge 44mm diameter.

Metal: Gilt, silver and bronze.

Ribbon: 38mm wide in the Federation colours being of three equal stripes of black, bright green and pale blue, separated by narrow dull yellow stripes. The ribbon of the 4th class is 32mm in diameter, whilst that of the medal omits the yellow.

Suspension: By a loop through a ring affixed to the uppermost point of the star.

Manufacturer: Spink and Sons Ltd., who between 1965 and 1966 produced the following:
                 1st Class – 6.
                 2nd Class – 16.
                 3rd Class – 36.
                 4th Class – 72.
                 5th Class – 100.

The order was awarded for distinguished service to the Federation on the following basis:

Military Division.

1st Class – "Hero", officers above the rank of brigadier, or the force commander if only a brigadier.

2nd Class – "Commander", officers of the rank of brigadier or full colonel.

3rd Class – "Officer", officers of rank of lieutenant-colonel and senior major.

4th Class – "Member", commissioned officers of the rank of junior major or below.

5th Class – Soldiers of the rank of warrant officer or below in recognition of specially distinguished or meritorious service.

Civil Division

1st Class – ministers, top-ranking officials and eminent officials for outstanding services.

2nd Class – senior officers of the administrative service, heads of professional and technical departments in the civil service, and prominent officials.

3rd Class – officers substantially holding super-scale posts in the civil service and officials of equivalent status.

4th Class – civil service officers of the scale C2 or above (if of under 10 years service the award is made for outstanding service), and officials of equivalent status.

5th Class – subordinate grades in the civil service and officials of equivalent status.

The order is known to have been awarded to the following British personnel:

1st Class	Sir Kennedy Trevaskis, High Commissioner.
2nd Class	Brigadier J. Lunt, C.B.E. Commander F.R.A.
	Brigadier G. Viner. Commander F.R.A.
3rd Class	Lt. Col. H.E.R. Watson, M.B.E., C.O. 2nd Battalion F.R.A.
	Lt. Col. H.J.W. Newton M.B.E., C.O. 3rd Battalion F.R.A.
	Major J.C.V. Todd, T.D. Training Battalion, F.R.A.
4th Class	Squadron Leader F.X. Grima. Medical Officer.
	Squadron Leader R.J.W. Martin. R.A.F Regiment.
5th Class	Sgt. R. Goodwins, R.A.F.
	Sgt. S. Kelly, R.E.M.E.

Other British personnel were recommended for awards but with the disintegration of the Federation it is uncertain if they were ever presented.

Gallantry Medal

Obverse:	A seven-pointed star.
Classes:	Two.
Metal:	1st Class – gilt.
	2nd Class – silver.
Ribbon:	Bright green.
Manufacturer:	Spink and Son Ltd.

Between 1965 and 1967 28 1st Class and 48 2nd Class awards were made. The medal was awarded for acts of outstanding gallantry by any member of the Federation, whether in combat or at peace. The two classes were as follows:
1st Class – "Hero". Awarded only for the acts of the most conspicuous bravery in circumstances of extreme danger.
2nd Class – "Companion". Awarded for acts of bravery of a very high order.
Award of the medal carried a cash grant of an equivalent of 200 Pounds Sterling for the 1st Class and 100 Pounds Sterling for the 2nd Class.

Military Service Medal

The medal was instituted to replace the British General Service Medal previously awarded to the Federal Forces for military operations in South Arabia. It would appear that this medal was never produced.

Long Service and Good Conduct Medals

Obverse:	(a) Federal Regular Army. In the centre two crossed daggers, hilts uppermost which surmount a horizontal scroll. Above the daggers an upturned crescent with a five-pointed star between its tips. (b) Federal Guard. A crescent with its tips to the right superimposed on which are two crossed rifles, a dagger in between. (c) Armed Police. A circular wreath with its base at "seven o'clock" superimposed on which is a truncheon, hilt lowermost.
Reverse:	Plain.
Size:	36 mm in diameter.
Metal:	Cupro-nickel.
Ribbon:	32mm wide of three equal stripes of black, bright green and scarlet, representing the Federal Guard, Federal Regular Army and the Armed Police.
Suspension:	By a bar affixed to the top of the medal.
Manufacturer:	Spink and Son Ltd. 200 were manufactured in 1965.

The medals were awarded to all N.C.O.'s of the Federation forces who had successfully completed 15 years of faithful service without serious disciplinary offence. A bar could be awarded on completion of each subsequent period of 5 years. Prior to the incorporation of Aden into the Federation of South Arabia the police were entitled to the Colonial Police Long Service Medal, which had been instituted in 1934. This was awarded to junior officers and below for 18 years full-time and exemplary service.

Glossary of Terms and Abbreviations

A.O.	Army Order.
A.P.	Aden Police.
A.P.L.	Aden Protectorate Levies.
A.P.T.G.	Aden Protectorate Tribal Guard.
Aqu'al	Camel hobble worn on top of the *imama*.
Bde.	Brigade.
B.E.M.	British Empire Medal.
Bn.	Battalion.
Bty.	Battery.
C.C.S.	Casualty Clearing Station.
Chaplis	Sandals.
D.C.L.I.	Duke of Cornwall's Light Infantry.
Durrie	Sleeping mat.
E.A.P.	Eastern Aden Protectorate.
Fd.	Field.
F.L.O.S.Y.	Front for Liberation of South Yemen.
F.N.G.	Federal National Guard.
Footah	Cotton kilt.
F.R.A.	Federal Regular Army.
G.O.C.	General Officer Commanding.
Golundauze	A Mughal word, golandaz, which means "a bringer of roundshot", indicating native artillery.
G.G.	Government Guards.
G.R.	Ground Reconnaissance.
H.A.C.	Honourable Artillery Company.
H.B.L.	Hadhrami Bedouin Legion
H.K.S.R.A.	Hong Kong Singapore Royal Artillery.
K.A.C.	Kathiri Armed Constabulary.
I.A.	Indian Army.
Imama	Cloth Arab headdress sometimes called *Kufiya* or *Shemagh*. Introduced by the Arab Legion.
I.O.D.	Indian Ordnance Depot.
I.S.F.	Indian State Forces.
Jambia	South Arabian curved dagger.
K.A.C.	Kathiri Armed Constabulary.
Katibas	Battalion.
Khulla	Conical part of *pagri*.

Kufiya	See *Imama*.
Kurta	Indian shirt.
Kuwash	Tribal pattern sandals of a type worn from Dahla to the Mushreq.
L.B.	Light Bomber.
L.M.G.	Light Machine Gun.
L.R.A.	Lahej Regular Army.
L.T.F.	Lahej Trained Forces.
M.A.R.A.	Military Assistant to Resident Adviser.
Mashedda	*Pagri* or Turban.
M.E.L.F.	Middle East Land Force.
M.M.G.	Medium Machine Gun.
M.R.A.	Mukalla Regular Army.
M.S.G.	Malay States Guides.
M.T.G.	Mahra Tribal Guard.
N.L.F.	National Liberation Front
Pagri	Turban.
Pk.	Park.
Q.A.C.	Qu'aiti Armed Constabulary.
Qamees	Arab shirt.
Q.F.	Quick Firing.
R.A.	Royal Artillery.
R.A.F.	Royal Air Force.
R.E.	Royal Engineers.
R.F.C.	Royal Flying Corps.
R.G.A.	Royal Garrison Artillery.
R.I.A.S.C.	Royal Indian Army Service Corps.
S.A.	South Arabian.
S.A.A.	South Arabian Army.
S&M.	Sappers and Miners.
S.A.P.	South Arabian Police.
Sedara	Headdress similar to British Army Service Hat (Side Hat) but with the hat badge to the front.
Shamla	The loose end protruding above the turban in the manner of a fan.
S.T.R.E.	Specialist Team Royal Engineers.
S.W.B.	South Wales Borderers.
T.G.	Tribal Guard.
Tarboosh	Fez.
W.A.P.	Western Aden Protectorate.

| W.T.G. | Wahidi Tribal Guard. |
| *Zamil* | War song. |

Bibliography

Primary Sources – Unpublished

Authors' Archives

Anon. *"A" Flight No. 10 Armoured Car Squadron. Aden Protectorate Levies.* Diary of events commencing 29th August 1956.

Anon. *Aden 1958–61.* N.d.

Anon. "Arabian Journey." Unpublished article, n.d.

Anon. "OP Outpost, Report on Ops by 3 APL 24 Apr – 27 May 60." Restricted, 3 APL Dhala, G/3/4, Aug 60.

Anon. *RAF Regiment and Associated Forces in Aden.* N.d.

Anon. *South Arabian Military Forces.* N.d.

Chaplain to the F.R.A. "Aden." Untitled articles, n.d.

Butt, C.R. "APL Reminiscence and Notes." Unpublished assorted notes and documents, 1992–98.

Butt, C.R. *Merta Road Incident June 1958.*

Ellis, J. "Unit Histories of the EAP, As Recalled by Jim Ellis." Unpublished assorted documents, 1986–99.

Moloney, R.J. Untitled article on West Aden Protectorate, November 3, 1962.

Thomas, C.B., D.S.O., M.C., Major-General Sandy, *History of 4 FRA.* N.d.

Tudor Pole, C.G. *Short History of the Aden Protectorate Levies.* (April 1928 – March 1944). N.d.

British Library, India Office Library and Records, London

R/20/A/164, Aden Irregular Horse.

R/20/B/180, Senior and Junior Tribal Guard Instructors Uniform Authorisation 1937.

R/20/B/180, Tribal Guards Instructors.

R/20/B/182, Dress Regulations for Gazetted Officers of the Aden Police, based on Colonial Police Service dress regulations for Gazetted Ranks, May 1938.

R/20/B/296, Letter from Commissioner of Police, Aden, to Legal Adviser, Aden, 3 August 1940.

R/20/B/1206, Extract from the minutes of a meeting held at the Secretariat regarding the duties of the Government Guards,1938.

R/20/G/318, Police and Police Arrangements, pp.17–19.

Directorate of Land Service Ammunition, Didcot

Starling, Major J.A. Unit Diary 1401 (Aden) Company.

Starling, Major J.A. Unit Diary 1402 (Aden) Company.

Starling, Major J.A. Unit Diary 1422 (Sultan Saleh's Hadramaut) Company.

MOD (R.A.F.) Historical Section, London

Anon. *RAF Regiment and Associated Forces in Aden*. N.d.

APL/S.2/7.Air, Appendix "B" to 540, "Report on an Escort to the Government Guard Nisab-Robat-Nisab. 15th June 1955." Background Information.

National Army Museum, London

54/Misc/6552, "APL, FRA, Insignia."

Public Relations and Information Department, Aden

"Operations Begin Against Dissidents in Western Aden Protectorate." Press Communiqué No.255/55, 10 July, 1955.

The War Office

"Grant of the General Service Medal for Service In the Arabian Peninsula." Special Army Orders No.9, 22nd February 1961. 68/General/9562 A.O. 9/ 1961.

Primary Sources – Published

Colonial Reports Annual 1937.

Colonial Reports Annual 1938.

"Composition of the Indian Expeditionary Forces", 01 February 1918 to 15 November 1919.

"Detail of Indian Units Serving out of India", 15 February 1920 to 01 May 1921.

Indian Army List, 1920 (for 45th Aden Rifles see pp.860).

The Inaugural Ceremony For The Federal Union Of The Amirates of Baihan And Dhala' And the Sultanates of 'Audhali And Fadhli And Yafa'I And The 'Upper 'Aulaqi Shaikhdom As The Federation Of Arab Amirates Of The South. Programme. Aden: Government Printer, 11 February 1959.

"Military Report on the Aden Protectorate." Simla: General Staff, 1915.

Port of Aden Annual 1953–54 (for Government Guards see pp. 19–21).

"Report by GOC, Aden, On The Operations of the Aden Field Force, 1st April – 18th August 1917." Simla: General Staff, 1917.

"Report by Major-General Sir G.J. Younghusband, K C.I.E., C.B., on the Action at Shaikh 'Othman 21st July 1915." Simla: General Staff, 1915.

"Summary of the Administration of Lord Curzon of Kedleston, Viceroy and Governor-General of India, in the Military Department, I. January 1899– April 1904. II. December 1904–November 1905" Simla: Government Central Branch Press, 1906.

Secondary Sources

Newspaper Articles and Magazines

Anon. "Aden. A Horrible Little War." *FlyPast*, October 1998, pp.116–120.

Anon. Letter on Berbera Landings, in *The Royal Pioneer*, No. 125, December 1975, pp. 31–32.

Ash, T. "Island Without Dogs." *The Wire Magazine*, June–July 1965, pp.170 – 173.

Cambridgeshire Weekly News, Thursday, November 7, 1985, pp.21. Article on Berbera Landings.

Eilts, H.F. "Along The Incense Roads of Aden." *National Geographic Magazine*, Vol. CXI, no. 2, February 1957.

Hutchinson, A.M.C. "The Hadrami Bedouin Legion." *Royal East Asiatic Society Magazine*, date unknown.

Lunt, James "Evolution of an Army." *Journal of the Royal United Services Institute*, parts 1 and 2, 1965.

Raw-Rees O. "The Awards of the Federation of South Arabia." *The Miscellany of Honours*, No.11, 1997, published by The Orders and Medals Research Society.

Raw-Rees O. "The Awards of the Sultanate of Lahej." *The Medal Collector, The Journal of the Orders and Medals Society of America*, Vol.47, no.8, October 1996.

Books

Anon. *The Historical Record of the Imperial Visit to India 1911*. London: John Murray, 1914.

Anon. *The History of the Corps of Royal Engineers Volume X (1946–1960)*. Chatham: Institution of Royal Engineers, 1986.

Anon. *The History of the Corps of Royal Engineers Volume XI (1960–1980)*. Chatham: Institution of Royal Engineers, 1993.

Anon. *The Punjab and the War*. Lahore: Suptdt. Govt. Printing, 1922.

Becke, A.F. *History of the Great War, Order of Battle Part 4*. London: H.M. Stationery Office, 1945.

Belhaven and Stenton, Lord. *The Uneven Road*. London, 1966.

Bousted, Hugh. *The Wind of Morning*. London: Chatto and Windus, 1971.

Corbally, Lt.Col. M.J.P.M. *The Royal Ulster Rifles 1793–1960*. Arbroath, 1960.

Corps of Signals Committee. *History of the Corps of Signals Volume I*. New Delhi: Corps of Signals Committee, Signals Directorate, A.H.Q., 1975.

Cunliffe, M. *The Royal Irish Fusiliers 1793–1968*. Oxford: Oxford University Press, 1970.

Drew, Lt. H.T.B. *The War Effort of New Zealand*. Auckland: Whitcombe and Tombs, 1923.

Gavin, R.J. *Aden Under British Rule 1839–1967*. London: C. Hurst and Co, 1975.

Graham, Brig. Gen. C.A.L. *The History of the Indian Mountain Artillery*. Aldershot: Gale and Polden, 1957.

Harper, S. *Last Sunset, What Happened In Aden*. London: Collins, 1978.

Hickinbotham, Tom. *Aden*. London: Constable and Company, 1958.

Ingrams, Harold. *Arabia and the Isles*. London: John Murray, 1966.

Johnston, Charles. *The View From Steamer Point*. London: Collins, 1964.

Joslin, E.C., A.R. Litherland and B.T. Simpkin. *British Battles and Medals*. London: Spink, 1988.

Ledger, David. *Shifting Sands*. London: Peninsular Publishing, 1983.

Lee, Air Chief Marshal Sir David. *Flight from the Middle East*. London: H.M.S.O., 1980.

Little, Tom. *South Arabia*. London: Pall Mall Press, 1986.

Lucas, Sir Charles. *The Empire At War, Volume V*. Oxford: Oxford University Press, 1926.

Lunt, James. *The Barren Rocks of Aden*. London: Herbert Jenkins Ltd. 1966.

Lunt, James. *Imperial Sunset, Frontier Soldiering in the 20th Century*. London: Macdonald, 1981.

Mehra, Major General K.C. *A History of the Army Ordnance Corps 1775–1974*. A.O.C. Directorate, 1980.

Macmunn, Lieut. Gen. Sir G. *Military Operations Egypt and Palestine, From the Outbreak of War with Germany to June 1917*. London: H.M. Stationery Office, 1928.

Nevins, E.M. *Forces of the British Empire 1914*. Virginia, 1992.

Nicolle, D. *Lawrence and the Arab Revolts*. London: Osprey, 1989.

Omissi, D.E. *Air Power and Colonial Control (The RAF 1919–1939)*. Manchester: Manchester University Press, 1990.

Paget, Julian. *Last Post: Aden 1964–1967*. Plymouth: Faber and Faber, 1969.

Rathbone Low, C. *History of The Indian Navy, Volume II*. Calcutta, 1877.

Reed, Stanley. *The King and Queen in India*. Bombay: Benneti, Coleman and Co., 1912.

Romer, Major C.F. and A.E. Mainwaring. *The Second Battalion Royal Dublin Fusiliers in the South African War With a Description of the Operations in the Aden Hinterland*. London: A.L. Humphreys, 1908.

Sandes, Lt. Col. E.W.C. *The Indian Sappers and Miners*. Chatham: Institution of Royal Engineers, 1948.

Singh, Inder. *History of the Malay States Guides, 1873–1919*. Penang: Cathay Printers, 1965.

Trevaskis, Sir Kennedy. *Shades of Amber*. London: Hutchinson, 1968.

Index